W9-ASV-663

Jimmy Black's
TALES FROM THE
TAR HEELS

Jimmy Black with Scott Fowler

SportsPublishingLLC.com

ISBN-10: 1-58261-982-4
ISBN-13: 978-1-58261-982-8

Publishers: Peter L. Bannon and Joseph J. Bannon Sr.
Senior managing editor: Susan M. Moyer
Acquisitions editor: Mike Pearson
Developmental editor: Travis W. Moran
Art director: K. Jeffrey Higgerson
Dust jacket design: Heidi Norsen
Interior layout: Kathryn R. Holleman
Photo editor: Erin Linden-Levy

Sports Publishing L.L.C.
804 North Neil Street
Champaign, IL 61820
Phone: 1-877-424-2665
Fax: 217-363-2073
www.SportsPublishingLLC.com

Printed in the United States of America

Library of Congress Cataloging-in-Publication Data

Black, Jimmy, 1960-
    [Tales from the Tar Heels]
    Jimmy Black's tales from the Tar Heels / Jimmy Black with Scott Fowler.
        p. cm.
    ISBN-13: 978-1-58261-982-8 (hard cover : alk. paper)
    ISBN-10: 1-58261-982-4 (hard cover : alk. paper)
    1. University of North Carolina at Chapel Hill--Basketball--History. 2. North Carolina Tar Heels (Basketball team)--History. 3. Black, Jimmy, 1960- I. Fowler, Scott. II. Title.
GV885.43.U54B53 2006
796.323'6309756565--dc22
                                    2006028396

Sincere thanks to my family and to all the players, coaches, friends, and associates who contributed to this book. Our journey together will never be the same, but, thankfully, it will never end.

—JB

CONTENTS

FOREWORD

As I sat reading this personal journal by Jimmy Black with Scott Fowler, I relived the journey of the North Carolina Tar Heels to the 1982 national championship of college basketball. This well-written narrative captures all of the excitement, the tension, and the stress of those games all over again. It's all here. You won't put it down.

But their story is most important for other reasons. These pages report the best in college sports in 1982. This Tar Heel team had great talent, to be sure. But it takes motivation, spirit, commitment, and discipline to harness such impressive individual players into the great team that they were. As this story reveals, they worked hard, they had fun, and most of all, they had Coach Dean Smith and his colleagues—Coach Bill Guthridge, Coach Eddie Fogler, and Coach Roy Williams.

In his time, Dean Smith was the best coach in intercollegiate basketball, not only because of his great skill and his inventiveness with the game, but because he always understood the importance of giving these young men the moral and personal compasses by which they would live their adult lives. That he succeeded is manifest by the records of useful citizenship each of his players has displayed during the last 40 years.

College sports is now struggling to regain control over its destiny. Being an entertainment industry is not its purpose. The consequences are too costly, as we see all too often now. This book reminds us that there is a better way—as this 1982 team made clear. Everyone who loves the game must now speak up and call for a return to the integrity and quality of the competition of 1982.

Jimmy Black and Scott Fowler point the way.

—William C. Friday
President Emeritus (1956-86)
of the University of North Carolina

ACKNOWLEDGMENTS

This book would never have been possible without the help of many people. Thanks to so many who devoted time and effort to helping myself and my co-author, Scott Fowler, get these stories from the 1981-82 season right.

First and foremost, thanks to God for His goodness and His grace.

To my wife, Amy, and my sons, Madison and Sean—thank you for giving purpose and adding normalcy to my life.

To my Uncle Charles and Aunt Melba—thank you for your love and support throughout my lifetime. To teammates of mine from other basketball squads, thank you for giving me the privilege of being able to call you "teammate." And thanks to UNC President William Friday—whom I've always told if he ran for President of the United States, this would be a much better world.

The book is mostly based on my own recollections of that championship season, supplemented with memories from many others associated with that team or with my own life—players, coaches, UNC officials, and media members.

The following folks, listed in alphabetical order, all answered questions for us and, in many cases, spent hours of their valuable time giving exclusive interviews for this book. We are so grateful to all of them:

Frank Barrows, Jimmy Braddock, John Brownlee, Rick Brewer, Chris Brust, Billy Cunningham, David Daly, Matt Doherty, Woody Durham, Cecil Exum, Coach Eddie Fogler, Lou Granda, Coach Bill Guthridge, Michael Jordan, Timo Makkonen, Warren Martin, Ralph Meekins, Tom Murray, Sam Perkins, Buzz Peterson, Lynwood Robinson, Coach Dean Smith, Dan Trotta, Coach Roy Williams, and James Worthy.

Thanks so much to our spectacular photographers for this book—Sally Sather and the late Hugh Morton. Their work during the 1981-82 season was wonderful, and they were so kind to provide us copies of it here. We can't thank them enough for their generosity, and you can witness their tremendous talent over and over throughout this book. Thanks also to Lance Richardson, who snapped our "author photo" on short notice one Friday morning at his studio in Chapel Hill.

Another word here about Hugh Morton, who died at age 85 in 2006. A few months before that, he had kindly provided dozens of his photos for us to choose from for this book, and he wouldn't accept payment for the use of any of them. They absolutely don't make them any better than Mr. Morton, whose legacy in this state as the owner of Grandfather Mountain, an environmentalist, a photographer, and a promoter of the state of North Carolina is unsurpassed.

Thanks to everyone at *The Charlotte Observer*, where Scott has worked since 1994, for allowing him to pursue this project on his own time and for maintaining such a detailed archive system of both that newspaper and the now-defunct *Charlotte News*. Thanks to John Drescher, managing editor of *The (Raleigh) News and Observer*, and all of his staff for allowing access to his newspaper's excellent files from the 1981-82 season. Thanks to Rob Reichley, the fine television producer, for his help in locating the original tape of the 1982 UNC-Georgetown championship game.

Thanks to other writers who came before us and chronicled this season in particular or North Carolina basketball in general. Art Chansky's *March to the Top*, written with Eddie Fogler and published shortly after the 1982 season concluded, was very helpful. Coach Dean Smith's memoir *A Coach's Life*, written with John Kilgo and Sally Jenkins, was also enlightening.

Former team manager David Daly's *One to Remember*—a 10-year retrospective of the 1982 team published in the early 1990s—also provided much insight. Daly, now a television producer, also gave us a look at several video files and the scrapbook he kept of the 1981-82 season, including pictures of the "on top of the bus" post-championship ride in Chapel Hill. Thanks, David.

Thanks to Kenny Duckett, a good friend, rest in peace. To Jim Boyle, mentor and friend, rest in peace. To Sid, Rick, Shake, King, and Cat—your friendships are invaluable. Godspeed.

Thanks to Steve Kirschner and Matt Bowers at the University of North Carolina sports information department for all their help with interviews, photos, research, and access.

Thanks also to those who helped as go-betweens in setting up some of these interviews, including John McMann, Mike Nelson, Ruth Kirkendall, and Linda Woods.

Thanks to Travis Moran, our editor at Sports Publishing, as well as the Sports Publishing man who first suggested this book—Mike Pearson—and all of the other professionals at SP. This is the third book Scott has written or co-written for SP, joining *Tales from the Carolina Panthers Sideline* (2004) and *North Carolina Tar Heels: Where Have You Gone?* (2005). He keeps going back for more because they are good people who care about producing quality work.

Finally, special thanks to all the fans of Tar Heel basketball—you are an extraordinary group. This book was written with the ultimate hope that all of you will enjoy it and better understand the magical ride of 1982.

INTRODUCTION

Twenty-five years ago, a group of special young men went on an incredible ride. I was part of that group—the starting point guard for North Carolina's 1981-82 national championship squad.

In this book, you'll learn things you never knew about that season and those young men. From the viewpoint of their senior co-captain, you'll find out what it was like to share the floor with James Worthy, Sam Perkins, Matt Doherty, and a freshman named Mike Jordan.

I will tell you honestly: I didn't think I would ever write a book about that incredibly memorable year. But then I was approached about this project by Sports Publishing and by my eventual co-author, *Charlotte Observer* sports columnist Scott Fowler. Scott is a 1987 North Carolina graduate himself and got his start in journalism as the sports editor of *The Daily Tar Heel*. He has always had a keen interest in Tar Heel basketball history and has covered Tar Heel basketball off-and-on for more than 20 years.

I entertained this idea primarily because commemorating the 25th anniversary of this team—letting people know how extraordinary this group of young men really was, both individually and collectively—is very important to me and for future fans.

We were just kids, ages 18 to 22, doing something that we loved. And fortunately, there was really nothing negative about that team. We had quality people. We did some great things, and that's what I want to share with people.

College athletics, unfortunately, has a negative connotation with some people. I want to let them know that there are still good and fun stories about college athletics out there. This is one of the better ones.

The 1982 team was one of the most well-known teams to ever play at North Carolina. I take absolutely no credit for that. As the senior point guard, I just tried to get our guys to win, to play hard, and to be in the right position.

Part of the '82 team's notoriety has to do with the fact that 1982 was Coach Dean Smith's first-ever national championship—that title we were finally able to win for him and for us.

I live in Durham now with my family. I'm in the Raleigh-Durham-Chapel Hill area—what we call the Research Triangle around here—a lot. I run into people all the time for one reason or another and many of them want to talk Carolina basketball. At some point, they always start asking me about the 1982 team. Then comes the question: "Who was the fifth starter on that team?"

Depending on who it was, they have always forgotten one of two people—either Matt Doherty or me. It's really funny. I get a chuckle out of it. They'll never forget Worthy, Perkins, or Jordan. I won't ever forget them, either, of course. But I also won't forget all the rest of my 1982 teammates—guys like Chris Brust, my college roommate, who formed a bond with me during the college years that will never be broken. And I won't forget the rest of that season.

I'm so fortunate that many of my former teammates and coaches participated in putting this book together as well. You're not just getting my memories in this book. Nearly everyone with a close association to our 1981-82 team—coaches, players, members of the media—consented to in-depth, exclusive interviews for this book as well. That interview list includes Coach Smith, the four other starters, and about 20 other folks. I am extremely grateful to them all, and this book is much richer for their participation.

The book is organized into more than 100 "tales"—short, behind-the-scenes anecdotes about the team. The wonderful pictures supplied mostly by Sally Sather and the late Hugh Morton—two fantastic photographers with generous souls—give the book even more life.

Although our ride to the 1982 title was wild and joyful, it was never easy. Not at all—actually, the ride started the year before. We had a terrific basketball team in the 1980-81 season. We didn't have Michael Jordan, but we did have great seniors in Mike Pepper, Pete Budko, Eric Kenny, and Al Wood, who scored 39 points in the NCAA semifinal against Virginia. But we lost to a great team, an Indiana squad led by Isiah Thomas, by 13 points in the 1981 NCAA final. Despite all we did that year, when the ride ended, it wasn't fun. Our stomachs hurt. The next year we wanted to take it to another level, and we ultimately did.

I've been involved with many basketball teams. Not only did I play in high school and college, but I was an assistant college basketball coach for a number of years as well. And what I can tell you was most unique on the 1982 team was that from Day One, everybody knew their roles. The roles were clearly defined by the coaches, and no one had any problem with them. As a consequence, everyone just went out and worked at getting better at what they did. I'm talking about *everybody*—it was beautiful.

And then there were the players. There were three guys on that team—Michael, Sam and James—who are either already in or really should be in the Basketball Hall of Fame in my opinion. That's incredible! What may be even more incredible is that all three worked their tails off all that season. Not only were they terrific players, they got after it every single day in practice. How could you not go hard when you saw how hard these guys practiced?

We finished 32-2 in 1981-82. I don't remember all the wins. I don't remember the scores except for our championship win over Georgetown—63-62—and that's only because I've seen that score in print so many times. I'm not a "score" guy. I'm a "win" guy, which is why I remember the losses. We lost to Virginia—with Ralph Sampson—and to Wake Forest during that season. Losses really ticked me off. We wanted to win every game. When preparedness meets talent, nothing matches that combination— and we had that. We had great coaches, great players, and most of all, *great* people.

Anyone who has ever played Carolina basketball knows that if you played in Chapel Hill, you have an identity with the program—forever. I was proud to come to UNC, proud that I was able to get in the game and able to represent my family in a positive way.

I've settled back near Chapel Hill these days. I work as a financial advisor with Raymond James Financial Services, with my office in Durham, North Carolina. I'm proud to call this area my home and happy to be in a business that caters to people, because I really enjoy people.

With two young children, I don't get to as many Carolina games as I'd like to anymore. But I'm proud of the current Tar Heels. I'm especially proud of the group that won the national title in 2005 because they have gone through turmoil that no other Carolina basketball player has ever gone through. I think people thought Coach Smith and Coach Bill Guthridge would be forever at Chapel Hill. When that changed, the dynamics of the program changed, and all of the young men who played from the 2000 season onward were affected the most. But to see them persevere and go on to accomplish their goals of another national championship for Carolina—that was probably the best season I've ever watched of college basketball.

The most fun I ever had playing? That's easy—1982.

Come with me on a stroll down Memory Lane—which would be called "Franklin Street" for many of us Tar Heel grads—as together we remember that unforgettable team.

—Jimmy Black

THE LAST 32 SECONDS

I t took 32 seconds for all of our lives to change that night in New Orleans.

It took more than six months to get there—starting with our practices in Chapel Hill in October 1981 and continuing through 33 other college basketball games.

But now we were down to the final 32 seconds of our season—the amount of time remaining when we called timeout in the 1982 North Carolina-Georgetown championship game. We were down by a single point, 62-61. Georgetown's Sleepy Floyd had just gotten into the lane, faked out half of our team, and hit a soft 10-foot jumper that bounced three times on the rim before falling.

On Floyd's basket, which came with 57 seconds remaining, the lead changed hands for the 16th time in the title game. It was extraordinary basketball. Five future first-round NBA draft picks and a couple of inarguable hall of famers were playing their hearts out on the court. Two future Hall of Fame head coaches were directing them. Both teams were playing superb defense, and yet, both teams were shooting over 50 percent as well.

But the last 32 seconds on the floor of the New Orleans Superdome is what everyone remembers most, including me. Any book about our 1982 season must start there.

There were 61,612 people in the Superdome that Monday night—March 29, 1982. They had paid either $16, $26, or $36 per ticket. They were getting one of the best deals in the history of college sports, even the ones who were watching in the $16 seats with binoculars from the crow's nest. I had never been involved in such a well-played, talent-drenched game.

We all knew we were smack in the middle of something special, but we put that thought far in the back of our minds. We just wanted to win—for the university, for Coach Dean Smith, for ourselves.

We needed one more basket. ...

THE TIMEOUT

Coach Smith had never won a national championship in six previous trips to the Final Four, and we badly wanted to get that monkey off his back. How these final 32 seconds played out would determine if we did it or not. Yet, Coach wasn't going to call timeout at first—a lot of times we didn't do that in similar situations, because we often got a better shot that way.

I was North Carolina's senior point guard and had been in the system for four years. I knew Coach Smith so well by then that I frequently signaled the play he wanted to my teammates before he had actually called it out to me. He sometimes joked in press conferences that season about what "Coach Black" had done on the floor.

After Floyd's basket, it was my job to dribble the ball up court. I did, slowly, and we gathered ourselves for one final push. We weren't in a hurry. Michael Jordan, Matt Doherty, and I started passing the ball around 35 feet from the basket, running down the clock, playing for the last shot.

Georgetown had dropped back in a zone and wasn't pressuring. I was ready to run our zone offense—I knew that's what Coach Smith would want. We hoped to get a good shot for James Worthy or Sam Perkins inside.

But Coach Smith conferred with one of our assistant coaches, Eddie Fogler, and decided "we didn't look right," in his words— maybe a little tight, maybe a little tired. So, with 32 seconds left, he called timeout.

And then the fun really began. ...

THE HUDDLE

Coach Smith started our timeout huddle by saying, as James Worthy remembered, "This is right where you want to be. This is just what we want. I'd rather be in our position than theirs right now." Then he told us we were going to run "our 'two game'"

We had a very close group of guys—that's one thing that made it special. We always seemed to be huddling up for one thing or the other—either on-court like here in the Final Four, or in one of our rooms at Granville Towers off-court. This shot also gives you a good sense of how short the uniform shorts were worn back then, and how high we pulled up our socks. *(Photo by Hugh Morton)*

against their zone, which he expected they would maintain after the timeout. That meant that Worthy would run down the lane; Perkins would follow behind him; and one of them might be open.

Then again, one might not be. As Coach Smith remembered in his interview for this book: "I knew John Thompson loved both those guys, particularly Worthy. He didn't want either one of them to beat us. So I knew James wasn't going to get it, but I thought Sam would get an easy shot."

As a backup plan, though, I would look for Jordan to shoot over the zone from the outside. It's easy to forget now, since Michael became the greatest player in the history of the game, but Jordan wasn't an exceptional outside shooter then. He had been taking 82 extra shots a game after most of our practices—82 in 1982—trying to improve his jumper.

But Coach Smith knew that it might come to that. As the huddle broke, he told Michael: "If it comes to you, knock it in."

THE SHOT—PART ONE

Michael said he had a vision on the team bus coming to the game that he would have a chance to sink the winning shot. He told a lot of folks about it later. But our first option on that team was always Worthy. He was our best player—in fact, in my mind, he and Phil Ford are the two best players in Tar Heel history.

So when I in-bounded the ball with 32 seconds left, I was thinking about James or Sam first. I threw it to Michael, who immediately threw it back to me. Then came James down the lane, with Sam trailing him. I looked—nothing. Georgetown had it all jammed up, with Ewing and his big body a huge presence in the middle of its 1-3-1 zone.

We needed to do something else. As we tried to probe the zone a little, we threw four straight passes, with me on either the giving or receiving end of all of them: to Michael, back to me, over to Matt Doherty, who was in traffic at the top of the foul-line circle, back again to me.

By now, just 18 seconds remained. All of our coaches were sitting down, and so were all the players on our bench except Jim Braddock. Everyone on Georgetown's bench, on the other hand, was standing.

Coach Smith thought we were moving too slowly, he would say later. He had wanted us to go ahead and get a fairly quick shot, so if we missed there would be a chance for a rebound or at least a foul of a Georgetown player and another possession. But I didn't want to rush it.

I took one quick dribble to the left, faking as if I might drive toward the basket, and the zone shifted a little toward me.

That was all I needed. I threw a skip pass over the top of the zone to Michael on the left side, 16 feet from the basket.

He shot immediately—no hesitation.

THE SHOT—PART TWO

Later, Michael would tell reporters that he closed his eyes midway through the shot and didn't actually watch the ball arc toward the goal. The rest, as you know, is history. It looked very good coming off his hand—even better when it swished through the net.

"I didn't see it go in," Michael said in the locker room right after the game. "I didn't want to watch it."

Michael understands the significance of the shot far more today than he did at the time, as he says today: "Obviously, that shot put me on the map in terms of how people viewed my skills on a national level. To me, it kick-started everything. In essence, it changed my name from 'Mike Jordan' to 'Michael Jordan.'"

Coach Smith would note later that Perkins wasn't blocked out under the goal, either. "If Michael's shot had gone just a little long, there's nobody over there with Sam," he said, "because they tried so hard to block out James. So Sam would have been the hero."

Instead, Michael was. He took the last pass I would ever throw in a college basketball game and turned it into my most well-known assist.

Our bench erupted, with Braddock in the lead, swinging a towel wildly. He had a head start of a couple of seconds on everyone else, but they caught up quickly. The shot had been right in front of them.

But there were still 15 seconds left in the game.

Georgetown had the ball with one timeout, but Coach Thompson didn't call it. Instead, they in-bounded to guard Fred Brown, and he started dribbling up court in a hurry.

THE DEFENSE

We all sprinted back in our "scramble" defense, where we tried to create some chaos by running at the dribbler and double-teaming. But if you look at photos and video of that night, we were scrambling, all right. It doesn't much look like we were in great position to play team defense—especially James Worthy, who for some reason was way out on the perimeter. I ran all the way back into the paint, where my one thought was, "No layups—can't let them get a layup!"

Immediately after the game, Coach Thompson would tell CBS that he thought the Hoyas were in great shape to score once he saw Worthy 25 feet from the basket. That same thought flashed through the mind of Sam Perkins—who suddenly was our only big man underneath.

"I ran back as fast as I could, because I knew Patrick Ewing would post up," Perkins explained. "But all of a sudden I saw Ed Spriggs, Georgetown's other big guy, on my right. And Ewing was right in front of me. How was I supposed to guard them both? How would I box them both out? I tried to yell to James, 'Get back! Get back!' I was 210 pounds at the time. Spriggs had to be at least 240, and you know how huge Ewing was. I didn't know what I was going to do."

Now there were eight seconds remaining. Brown stopped dribbling and thought about getting the ball to Floyd again, who looked open for a second. But then Jordan made the subtle play that no one pointed out after the game. Michael took one quick step to the left. It was another in a series of fine defensive moves for Michael—for the first time in his North Carolina career following this game, the coaches would give him our "Defensive Player of the Game" award.

With Michael's sudden step, Brown's passing lane suddenly closed—and he started to panic.

THE STEAL

Brown was dead set on *not* taking the shot that would determine the national championship. He had shot only twice the entire game—Ewing had already taken 15 shots, and Floyd had taken 16. One of them needed the ball. When Jordan closed down the passing lane, Brown thought he saw another Georgetown player out of the corner of his eye.

And remember, by that point, Brown had picked up his dribble. He could have signaled for a timeout. Ironic, isn't it? On this same floor, 11 years later, Michigan's Chris Webber would signal for a timeout he didn't have in another famous NCAA title game involving the Tar Heels. This time, Brown had a timeout, but didn't use it.

James was an expert at cutting off passing lanes. He would gamble in a heartbeat because he was so amazingly quick. When James saw Brown stop dribbling and hold the ball, he gambled again.

"When Brown did that," Worthy said, "I actually made a bad defensive move and went for a pump fake. I went so far out—way past where our normal defense would set up—that I was actually *behind* Fred Brown. He must have panicked and thought I was on his team. He threw it right to me."

On national television, play-by-play man Gary Bender saw Brown's mistake and roared: "Oh, he threw it to the wrong man! He threw it to Worthy!"

On the Tar Heels' radio network, as Worthy gratefully took Brown's errant pass and dribbled toward Georgetown's goal, play-by-play man Woody Durham screamed: "How 'bout them Heels! They are the national champions!"

Billy Packer, on CBS, had nearly the same reaction. "It's over! It's over!" he shouted on-air.

There was one small problem—it wasn't over. Worthy, who had never met a dunk opportunity he didn't like, finally became acquainted with one.

THE FREE THROWS

Worthy caught Brown's pass with five seconds left. After that, he remembered in his interview for this book: "I was a leader on the floor on that team, and our leading scorer as well. But I will admit that, in a strange situation like that, I panicked. I didn't want to screw up anything. What if I tried to dunk and missed, and they got the ball back? That's what I was thinking. I saw Michael Jordan coming down the middle—he was open—and I thought about passing to him. But ultimately, I did the safe thing. I just veered to the left. I thought maybe I could make it to zero, that the clock would run out and the game would be over."

With two seconds left, however, Georgetown's Eric Smith caught up to Worthy and fouled him. The officials called it an intentional foul. Rather than the one-and-one, which was used indefinitely at that time in college basketball once a team got into the bonus, Worthy would have two shots.

In his radio seat on the second row of the Superdome floor, Woody Durham regrouped.

"I was like thousands of Carolina fans watching and listening," Durham said. "I was ready to start celebrating. But then I looked at Coach Smith and saw him up and motioning everybody over to him. I said to myself, 'Hey, he doesn't think this is over. I better calm down.'"

To Worthy, Coach Smith said simply: "Make them."

Coach Thompson then called a timeout. It was Georgetown's final one—the timeout Brown could have used. It meant Georgetown would have no time to set up a play if Worthy missed the second free throw.

With 0:02 on the clock, Worthy's first free throw bounced off the rim and out.

"At that point," Coach Smith would say 25 years later, "I made a mistake. I should have told James to go ahead and miss the second one on purpose, too, to make it harder for them to get off a good shot."

It still worked out that way. The genesis of the "Big Game James" nickname really started in the Superdome, not with the L.A. Lakers. James scored 28 points in the game—almost double his regular-season scoring average—and made 13 of 17 shots. Bill

Guthridge, our chief assistant coach at the time, would later call it one of the greatest college games ever played by any individual player.

But Worthy had an Achilles heel that night. Worthy had missed four of his six free-throw attempts as he set up for that last one, which missed, too, banging off the front rim. Georgetown rebounded the ball and quickly got it to Floyd. He was 55 feet from the rim, not even to half court, when he had to launch it just before the buzzer.

Still, the shot was on line. Coach Smith had a good angle to see that, but couldn't judge how far Floyd had slung it.

"I saw it was on course," Smith said, "and I just about had a heart attack."

Thankfully, he didn't. The ball was 12 feet short. Perkins caught it in the air, immediately fired it back over his head, and ran toward the rest of us, looking for someone to hug.

By that time, the court was a jubilant, Carolina-blue mess. Coach Smith and Coach Thompson hugged. Then Coach Smith and I found each other and shared a really nice moment. "Jimmy was the first player I hugged. I told him I loved him. He told me that he loved me, too," said Dean Smith.

"IF I'D HAD A RUBBER BAND"

After his turnover, Brown was consoled by teammates. His coach, John Thompson, put a fatherly arm around him and also hugged him and patted him on the back. He would say later in the press conference that Brown had "just made a mistake" and had won far more games for Georgetown than he lost. Thompson would say in a postgame interview with CBS: "It's just one of those human errors, there's nothing in the world you can do about it."

Shortly after the game, Brown gave his side of why he threw the ball to Worthy: "I picked up my dribble and that killed it. At that point, I should have called timeout. But I saw Eric Smith open on the left baseline. But they overplayed, so I looked for Pat. They were all covered, so I tried to pass it [to Floyd]. But it wasn't him. If I'd had a rubber band, I would've pulled it back."

THE AFTERMATH

Coach Smith was walking to his hotel from the Superdome after all of his media and team obligations were finally over.

"In the hotel lobby, the very first guy I saw was in a Carolina hat," Coach Smith recounted. "I didn't know him. He said, 'Coach, Coach! Couldn't Worthy have made at least one of those foul shots?'"

"Talk about looking a gift horse in the mouth," Coach Smith thought for a second. Then he realized the man must have bet on the game. Carolina had been slightly favored, so Worthy missing the free throws meant that the Tar Heels didn't cover the spread. James, in fact, eventually would receive a few angry letters back at Chapel Hill from Las Vegas bookies and others who had lost money on the game. Even today, someone occasionally reminds him of it.

Coach Smith was ready to see his family that night, though, and he didn't want to get in a discussion about Worthy's free throws. "That'll teach you not to gamble," Coach Smith said, and kept walking.

2

SECRETS OF
1982

That Georgetown game was magical. Part of its power, of course, is that so many people saw it. Those images are embedded in your mind and in mine as well.

In this chapter, I want to tell you much more about the figures that were on your television that night in 1982, or years later on some NBA game or ESPN Classic. You know the names of many of the players on our 1981-82 team. Its star quality—and I'm not including myself in that phrase one bit—is one reason it has such staying power.

There's a lot you don't know about that season 25 years ago, and the cast of characters that made it happen. So before we go any further, I need to let you in on some of the behind-the-scenes stuff. I want you to understand who these guys were so you appreciate later how far we all came. And I want you to understand some of the things we did together as a team. It's 25 years later, after all.

TWILIGHT ZONE

Our favorite television show as a team that season was an eerie science-fiction series that had stopped producing new shows about the time most of us were in diapers. But we loved *The Twilight Zone*, with its weird twists, unusual characters, and unfamiliar surroundings. It was a great escape for all of us.

The place we usually watched was in the room I shared with Chris Brust. WUNC, the public television station, aired two reruns of *Twilight Zone* episodes, back-to-back without commercials, every weeknight starting at 11 p.m. That's an ideal time for college-student television.

It was unbelievable how so many of us players on the 1981-82 team was hooked on the show. *The Twilight Zone* ran from 1959 to 1964, with Rod Serling as the narrator and principal writer. There were 156 episodes altogether, and we saw almost every one of them—many of them twice. Guys would actually go out on Franklin Street, come back into Granville so they could watch the episodes from 11 p.m. to midnight, and then go back out again!

It's been so long since I've seen a *Twilight Zone* episode that I can't remember my favorite now. But Chris Brust ended up watching the show again as an adult with his own kids. He can still tell you about the one called "Talky Tina"—a 1963 episode that starred Telly "Kojak" Savalas as the father of a girl who got a talking doll.

Kojak didn't like the doll, and the doll didn't like him. Eventually, he tried to get rid of the doll, but the doll ended up slyly getting in his way near a staircase and tripped him. Kojak died on the fall down the stairs, and the doll soon warned the little girl's mother: "You better be nice to me!"

We loved that sort of stuff. It was so different from our regular lives. It was just a terrific show.

THE ROSTER—PART ONE

Our entire team lived together in Granville Towers on 125 West Franklin Street that year. Later, Coach Smith would let upperclassmen move off-campus, but that came right after I left. That's one reason why we were such a close team and did things like watch *Twilight Zone* together—we were just around each other so much. We had most of a hall to ourselves on the first floor of Granville South, living two to a room.

Jeb Barlow transferred in from Louisburg Junior College and earned a scholarship. He was a very good player that fit in well for us. He was from Fuquay-Varina, North Carolina, and we called him "Country."

Jim Braddock was our backup at both guard spots. He was a junior and just about the strongest guy on our team. His nickname

1981-82 UNC BASKETBALL ROSTER

Name	Yr	Ht	Pos
JEB BARLOW	SR	6-8	F
JIMMY BLACK	SR	6-3	G
JIM BRADDOCK	JR	6-2	G
JOHN BROWNLEE	FR	6-10	F/C
CHRIS BRUST	SR	6-9	F
MATT DOHERTY	SO	6-8	F
CECIL EXUM	SO	6-6	F
MICHAEL JORDAN	FR	6-6	G/F
TIMO MAKKONEN	FR	6-11	C
WARREN MARTIN	FR	6-11	F/C
SAM PERKINS	SO	6-9	C
BUZZ PETERSON	FR	6-4	G
LYNWOOD ROBINSON	FR	6-1	G
JAMES WORTHY	JR	6-9	F

HEAD COACH–DEAN SMITH
CHIEF ASSISTANT–BILL GUTHRIDGE
ASSISTANT–EDDIE FOGLER
PART-TIME ASSISTANT–ROY WILLIAMS

was "Daddy," because sometimes when you asked him what happened, he'd say, "Your daddy did it." He said it all the time. He ended up subbing in for Michael Jordan and me when either of us needed a breather.

John Brownlee was a freshman that year. He was a nice guy from Fort Worth, and he never quite got Texas out of his system. He didn't play much for us, but when he transferred back to Texas, he became the Southwest Conference player of the year in 1986.

Chris Brust was my roommate and my best friend on the team. We came in the same year as freshmen. You won't even believe how good Chris could have been had he not been injured for most of his career.

Matt Doherty, a future coach at North Carolina, is the first starter we come to on this list. He was a terrific player with great savvy. Although he was 6-feet-8, he really could have played point guard. Matt seemed to do everything right—he was always studying, and he didn't go out with us on Franklin Street that much because of that. Cecil Exum, another one of our teammates, sometimes called him "Prince Charles" because of the way he acted. Matt was very proper. Exum was a sophomore that year, and he was unstoppable in practice. He didn't get into the games much, but, in practice, he was amazing—slashing, shooting, whatever he wanted. Matt could not guard that kid in practice to save his life.

THE ROSTER—PART 2

Michael Jordan was our only freshman starter that season. He was athletic and raw, funny and cocky. We used to always kid him because Buzz Peterson won North Carolina High School Player of the Year over him when they were both seniors. I would say, "Why are you so cocky, Michael? You weren't even the best player in your state. What you talking about?"

Buzz was a better pure shooter than Michael when they were freshmen. Michael was very talented, but we didn't have any idea what he had. To see how he evolved—hey, I'm amazed to this day. Those two were roommates.

Timo Makkonen was our big kid from Finland, and he had a surprisingly good sense of humor, too. One night, he had just gotten a new car. Lynwood Robinson and myself were in my room watching television. It was snowing outside. Timo ducked his head in and said, "Hey, Lynwood, you want to go for a ride in my new car?" Lynwood said, "Sure." They drove around the corner—to a covered parking lot right behind Franklin Street near Spanky's. Timo didn't want to get snow on his car. "Okay, ride's over," Timo said. Lynwood and Timo had to walk back to Granville, and Lynwood was *hot*. Timo had said he was going to take him for a ride, and he sure did.

Warren Martin was a 6-foot-11 freshman whom we called "Cricket." That's because he had this little head on top of this great big body. I take credit for that nickname. Warren and Timo lived together in Granville—"the world's largest roommates," some called them.

This is our official team picture from 1981-82. Everyone in this picture knew their role perfectly, from players to coaches to team managers and doctors. The picture was taken on the floor of Carmichael Auditorium, our home court that season. The Dean Smith Center wasn't open yet. *(Photo courtesy of UNC)*

Sam Perkins, of course, was one of our very best players. People thought he didn't work that hard because he was so graceful. Let me tell you, no one worked any harder than Sam did. We recruited Ralph Sampson back around that time. In fact, Ralph told me point-blank during his visit he was coming to North Carolina. And had we gotten Ralph, we probably never would have recruited Sam. Now that I look back on it, thank you, Ralph, for going to Virginia—thank you so much. Because if you had come here, I never would have gotten to know Sam the way I did.

As for Lynwood Robinson, who would later transfer to Appalachian State and have a fine career there, he really missed his calling. He should have been a comedian. He can impersonate anyone 30 seconds after hearing a voice. He's one of the funniest guys I ever met. And he loved music—all types of music. When you rode with him in a car and heard a song, you could bet he knew the singer.

Lynwood provided the soundtrack for most of the season. Michael lugged around the film projector—that was always a freshman's job, too, and usually the one given to a player who was both very good and very brash about his own ability. Michael fit both counts. Lynwood provided the tunes on this big radio-tape player he had.

I've saved the best for last—in terms of playing ability, anyway. James Worthy was so good in 1982 that he deserves his own section in this introduction.

"STICKING" IT TO THEM

Was Michael Jordan the best player on our team in 1982? I get asked that a lot. No, he wasn't—not even close. Remember, he was a freshman—cocky, creative under the basket, but still raw. His body hadn't developed. He wasn't our second-best player, either— that was Sam Perkins.

Our best player was James Worthy.

James went 13 for 17 against Georgetown in that championship game, made the big steal, scored 28 points, and was the Final Four's MVP. But we all knew how great he was long before that happened. In crunch time that season, if you watch the tapes, you will see that every time it was close, I called "Fist Four," which meant I was coming to "Stick"—I was going to James. He was our 'four' man, our power forward, and I was going to him.

Even coming out of a timeout sometimes, Coach Smith would call something and I'd just sort of overrule it. I'd walk over to James just before play started again and say "Stick, I'm coming to you." And you know what? Coach didn't get mad, because we scored.

When that thing got tight? "Stick, I'm coming, baby." And he knew it. He'd just give me one of those looks like, "Yeah, bring it— bring it in here, and I'll score," which made me the happiest man in the country.

James Worthy was unguardable, really. I never saw anybody who was 6-feet-9 that could run like he could and had hands like he did. He was a freak, really—a *freak*. I've never seen anything like that.

He could play anywhere he wanted to play, and that was the beauty of that team. Matt, Michael, Sam, and James were all so versatile. I was really the only guy who played one position, a traditional position, at point guard. The others could all play two or three spots. They were so talented it was scary. I didn't realize it at the time, of course—we were just playing basketball. But I'll tell you this: I could put together a NBA squad with those four, in their primes, as starters, and I think we'd be all right. They could play, and they had a feel for the game. Not only were they talented, they *knew* the game.

Yet, none of them was better than "Stick."

BUZZ AND MJ

One of the most interesting relationships on our 1981-82 team had to be the one between two of our own freshmen—Michael Jeffrey Jordan and Robert "Buzz" Peterson. You know a lot about Michael by now, but maybe you don't remember Buzz as a player. He grew up in Asheville and acquired the nickname "Buzz" very early. His older sister nicknamed him after a cartoon character, a bee that was called "Brother Buzz."

Buzz was a great shooter and a basketball junkie from the beginning. He once painted 10 green stripes on his driveway with his mother's brush and then shot hundreds of shots from each stripe on his backyard goal. He was a superb high-school basketball player—so good, in fact, that, as we reminded Michael all the time, Buzz was the 1981 North Carolina "Prep Player of the Year" over Jordan.

"Michael always ribs me on that," Peterson said. "But although he was a very good athlete back then in high school, he wasn't a totally polished basketball player yet. And his body wasn't mature."

Buzz would later become a successful college head basketball coach—he was head coach at Tennessee for four seasons and is now the head coach at Coastal Carolina near Myrtle Beach, South Carolina. But his career with us was plagued by leg and knee injuries. He did play for us in the '82 championship game against Georgetown, though. He got in for only seven minutes, but made a steal that resulted in a Worthy dunk. They still show that clip sometimes during March Madness promos.

Of course, Michael and Buzz were close friends in college, and both learned golf there—future pro Davis Love III was their mentor on UNC's Finley Golf Course. And Buzz used to go see Jordan every year while Jordan was still playing in the NBA.

"I'll never forget Michael telling me, during about the third year in the pros, that people used to tell him he had chosen the wrong school because I was going to play in front of him," Buzz said. "He told me in practice that the only thing he thought of that first year when we were both at Carolina as freshmen was, 'Be better than Buzz. Be better than Buzz.'"

Jordan, of course, was better than everybody. He and Buzz were longtime college roommates at Granville and used to borrow each others' clothes all the time. They both wore size-13 shoes, but Jordan's feet were so wide that he would stretch Peterson's loafers all out of shape.

"If you ever make it big," Peterson told him, "you're going to keep me in dress shoes the rest of my life."

For about 15 years, that was true. Whenever Buzz went to see Jordan, he'd also go into Jordan's closet and, with MJ's permission, pick out two pairs of dress shoes to take home with him.

"I don't do that anymore," Peterson said. "I can afford my own shoes now."

THE 40-YARD DASH

Each year we were timed in the 40-yard dash. It was part of our preseason-conditioning program, which Roy Williams supervised in 1981-82 as part of his assistant coaching duties.

To make it more competitive, we made it a race, running in groups of three. The guys with the slower times were eliminated. Finally, three players were left that season. Any guesses as to whom they were?

James Worthy, Michael Jordan, and Buzz Peterson.

So we had a 6-foot-9 guy, a 6-foot-5 guy, and a 6-foot-3 guy racing in the final.

The order they finished in might surprise you, too. Worthy, besides being our best player that season, was also our fastest in a sprint. James was an incredible athlete, I'm telling you. And that day, he finished first.

"I'm pretty quick from zero to 60," Worthy said recently, laughing at the memory of that 40, "always have been."

Buzz was second, Jordan third.

"It was a great moment," said Peterson, recalling that race. "And now still it allows me to tell Michael: 'I beat you out for high school player of the year in North Carolina; I beat you in the 40-yard dash when we were freshmen; and I could always out-swim you.'"

Coach Bill Guthridge remembers that race, too—and he remembers what happened the next season, too. "Michael was so much faster when he was a sophomore that he just blew Buzz away. It wasn't even close."

MIKE VERSUS MICHAEL

We mostly called Michael Jordan "Mike" when he came to campus at first. But by midseason, his first name started to change—at least publicly. The newspapers and television commentators started referring to our starting freshman as Michael Jordan, the name he would later make famous. Most times, he was still "Mike" to us, but not to the world at large.

Our sports information director at UNC at the time was Rick Brewer, and he was the one who made the switch. Here's how he described it: "When Jordan came in, the players referred to him as Mike. So that's what I went with in the media guide, which we had to publish early, before the season even started."

"But the more I hung around the players I realized that half of them called him Michael and half called him Mike," Brewer continued. "Now Coach Smith is very specific about these sorts of things—he's one of the very few people in the world who calls Charlie Scott 'Charles.' He uses proper names a lot. So I went to see Jordan about it. I walked downstairs into the locker room at Carmichael, and he was the only kid there, just lacing up his shoes."

Brewer approached the freshman and explained the name quandary.

"So do you want to be Mike or Michael?" Brewer asked.

"I really don't care," Jordan said. "Which one would you say?"

"Michael really sounds like it has a better ring to it," Brewer said. "It sounds like a name that flows easier off your tongue when you say it."

"Okay," Jordan said, without giving it any more thought, and he walked out the door to practice.

SKATING ALONG

That team was big into nicknames. Even some members of the staff had them. We called one of our senior managers, David Daly, "Dip." That's because David was in charge of the meal money, and we were always wanting him to dip into his zippered moneybag so we could get something to eat.

I nicknamed our head athletic trainer, Marc Davis, "Skate." Marc has been doing that job for a long time now—he still is the trainer today, and he started the job in the 1977-78 season. One day, James Worthy got hurt in practice. Marc was one of most easygoing guys in world, and he was walking out there pretty slow. Coach Smith must have been having a bad day. He says, "Marc, my gosh, can't you walk out there any faster?"

From that point on, Marc went faster, and I started calling him 'Skate' because he started moving like he was on skates, with his hands behind his back.

A FINE FRENCH TIE

Coach Guthridge never got enough credit for his role as Coach Smith's chief assistant for all those years. That's one reason I was so glad was hired as North Carolina's head coach from 1997 to 2000. Coach Guthridge led North Carolina to two Final Fours in his three years as head coach, which helped some fans understand how good of a coach he always was.

Coach Smith got all the credit from most people in my playing days, and he's an absolutely tremendous coach. But I tell you what: North Carolina, as people know it, *would not be* North Carolina if Coach Guthridge was not a member of that staff. No one else could have filled that role as Coach Smith's right-hand man.

I always liked Coach Guthridge. He was extremely honest and supportive—like a parent. If you did the right thing, he praised you. If you did the wrong thing, he scolded you. If I had a problem, though, I went to Coach Guthridge. And he was so funny—people don't realize that, but he has this real dry sense of

All four of the coaches on the 1981-82 UNC staff became head coaches if they weren't already. From left to right, that's Roy Williams, Eddie Fogler, Bill Guthridge and Coach Dean Smith. *(Photo courtesy of UNC)*

humor. One day we were going on a trip, and I must have had a nice tie on, because he walkd up to me and said, "Hey, nice tie." I think it was a Pierre Cardin. He was standing there, still looking at me, and I said, "Coach, you have on a nice tie too." Which he didn't—but I was trying to be nice.

Coach Guthridge flipped it around so he could read the label and then, in a real bad French accent, said, "It's a J.C. Penn-ay."

One Sunday before the 1981-82 season started, we had a Sunday practice. The players didn't really want to be there. We had practiced hard all week, and we wanted to relax and watch some

NFL football. The coaches realized this somehow. Early in the practice, before we really got going, Coach Smith said to Coach Guthridge: "Hey, Coach, have you heard any football scores?"

"Sure have," Coach Guthridge said, "20-10, 18-3, 24-21, 17-14 ..." no team names, just random scores. It broke us all up. Suddenly, our workout didn't seem monotonous anymore, and we went out and had an excellent practice.

RUNNING AT SIX A.M.

Coach Guthridge was also a dedicated jogger. He ran several miles most mornings at six a.m. All of us accompanied him at one time or the other—although not by choice. That was one of the punishments we could receive. If we messed up—not showing up for class, for instance—we would get the distinct privilege of meeting Coach Guthridge outside Carmichael at six a.m.

For those who don't know, Carmichael was right in the middle of campus. (The Dean Smith Center, on the other hand, is way down on the south edge of campus, but it hadn't been built when we were in school.)

Coach Guthridge would lead the offending player on a jog that was mostly downhill for about a mile and a half. Then, just when the player was starting to get tired, you'd turn around and start running back to Carmichael. That last mile and a half—almost all of it uphill—could really hurt you.

"I ran alone most of the time during that 1981-82 season," remembered Coach Guthridge. "There weren't that many times someone had to run with me. First of all, that was a good group—they mostly did what they were supposed to. And once they did it with me once, they really didn't want to do it ever again."

3

GROWING UP, GETTING BETTER

This chapter takes you through the early years of my life, from growing up in The Bronx through the first two years of my college career at North Carolina. I'm okay if you skip ahead and go straight to the stories about the other guys on the team or about the 1981-82 season. I truly am. Being in the spotlight is never something I have sought—not on the basketball court and not in life. Now I did like to run things on the basketball court— don't get me wrong. But I didn't need the publicity. I just wanted the wins. Still, if you want to know where I'm coming from— literally—I'll get to Chapel Hill and all we did there. But I need to start in New York.

MY FAMILY

I grew up in The Bronx, born on November 20, 1960. It was hot. Everything was concrete, and I lived in the projects. Now every time I read a story about someone coming from the projects, you always keep hearing about how these guys are poor. But I grew up in the projects, and I didn't think we were poor at all. I always thought I had a whole bunch. As a kid, I got a bicycle, a moped, all of that stuff. I also was blessed to have many great friends, too. As an only child, you need a lot of friends.

My father's name was Lee. My mother's name was Joyce, but the family called her Marie. They were disciplinarians, but they allowed me to grow as well. When I was young, I thought I was smarter than them, as most teenagers do at various times. Looking back, I wasn't even close.

My mother and father both worked. My dad was in the publishing business, and my mother was an administrative assistant. So I was a latchkey kid. I would come home from school, let myself in, change and rush downstairs to play.

We did all the normal things that kids do—played baseball, football, stickball, basketball, tag, the whole nine yards. We had a basketball court and a baseball field, but most of the time the activity was right out in the street.

CATHOLIC SCHOOL UPBRINGING

Although my family didn't have much money, I went to private Catholic schools all the way through until I got to Carolina. My mother and father made a huge, tremendous sacrifice and afforded me the opportunity to get a great education, something for which I'm extremely grateful.

In high school, I went to Cardinal Hayes in the Bronx. I rode the train there—that's what we called the subway—every day. It was an all-boys school, about 350 to 400 kids altogether at the time. The school was maybe 20-percent black, and there was no real racial tension at all. My high school was wonderful. Black kids hung out with white kids and Hispanic kids. Priests taught most of our classes, but we also had lay teachers as well. We had to wear a shirt, tie, and coat every day.

I had two jackets in my locker and kept my ties in there, too. I'd get to school and throw on my jacket and my tie. There was really no peer pressure as far as how you looked, because no girls went to school there.

FREDDY AND NEW YORK

My full name is James Frederick Black, but everyone in North Carolina calls me "Jimmy." In high school, I was James Black—I didn't go with "Jimmy" until I got to college.

However, my family calls me "Freddy" to this day. All my friends from New York call me that, too. If I'm walking down the street, and I hear somebody say that, I know immediately they are from New York. No question about it. The only one who calls me Freddy outside of New York friends and family is Phil Ford. We went to New York together once, and I guess he heard it, so he adopted that, too.

'A 100-WATT SMILE'

In my freshman year at Cardinal Hayes High, I still didn't know whether I was a very good basketball player or not. The first time I realized I might have the abilities was during the tryouts for the freshman team. The coach was Danny Trotta—he was only 24 years old at the time and has remained a very good friend of mine to this day. He lives in the Charlotte area now.

Coach Trotta gave me a look that I'll never forget during one of the drills we were doing. The look said, "Man, you're a pretty good player." He had this smile on his face, and that made me feel better. He didn't know me from Adam, but he had noticed me. I thought maybe things were going to work out.

Coach Trotta remembers that freshman team, too. "A lot of the Catholic schools around there recruited kids to come play at that time. We didn't—we just took whoever showed up. So you didn't know what you were getting. I had 70 kids come try out that year, and I could only take 15. Tons of them could play. This was a fairly rough area in the South Bronx—some of the kids listened to you, some didn't.

"To this day, I will always remember this skinny kid with a 100-watt smile. I found out quickly this was Jimmy Black—always smiling, always having a good time. And after about two weeks, I realized he was one of the quickest people I'd ever seen in my life. On defense, Jimmy was the most incredible player I'd seen at that age. He could just lock somebody up for a five-second violation. He was a kid who listened, too. He was a leader, but he always wanted to fit in. He never wanted to be the star, even though he had more talent than anybody else on that team."

"One of our biggest wins that year was against Power Memorial—a real powerhouse of a basketball school, the place where Lew Alcindor [who would change his name to Kareem Abdul-Jabbar] had once gone," continued Coach Trotta. "They had a mystique about them. It went all the way down to their

I'm not sure who I was waving at in this picture, but I was happy to see them. I've always tried to have fun with basketball—you can't make it too serious. *(Photo by Sally Sather)*

uniforms. We had hand-me-downs, but their freshman team had these really great uniforms. It wasn't Power Memorial's best team ever by any means. But our guys—a lot of them seemed intimidated about those uniforms. Seriously. I remember getting mad and saying, 'What's the deal with the uniforms, guys? You know these players. You're better than these players. The uniforms don't matter. ' We went out and beat them by 20. Jimmy was the leader. They couldn't trap us or press us—we were just too quick."

'A CERTAIN JOY'

Even as a high school kid, I always liked to pass. There was always a certain joy for me in making assists. One of my best friends was Teddy Murphy, and he and I would go play in tournaments throughout the city together. I wanted Murphy on my team because I loved throwing him the ball. He could finish, and I enjoyed watching him score.

As a player throughout high school and college, I did throw some fancy passes. They weren't something I particularly tried to do, it was just something that happened in the flow of the game.

I was always a better basketball player than I was an athlete. Raymond Felton, for instance, is both an extremely good basketball player and a terrific athlete. Felton could probably have been a quarterback, too, the way he can zigzag around. I never could have done that. That's the distinction.

I could dunk, although I rarely did. But the thing that separated me from some of the others was that I had a feel for the game that you can't really teach.

LOCK HIM UP

My high school teammate in The Bronx—Lou Granda—tells many good stories about our days as teammates at Cardinal Hayes High. His memory of those days is sometimes better than mine.

"I was a year ahead of Jimmy in school," Granda said. "So the first time I met him, I was on the jayvee team, and Jimmy was on the freshman team. Our high school coach told me to go down and work out with the freshman team to give Jimmy a workout. I thought it was more like I was going to teach him something. But he actually ended up teaching me. I walked away from that experience saying, 'I need to transfer!' I really did. And I did consider transferring. He was just too quick, too good. But we very quickly developed a mutual respect for each other, and, to this day, we're great friends."

Continued Granda: "There were times in the lay-up line that Jimmy would look at the opposing guard—the one he knew he would be facing the whole game—and make a motion. It was the motion of padlocking a gate. And he'd say, out loud: 'I'm going to lock him up. '

"Jimmy just had all the confidence in the world. He had confidence, and he could back it up. He took every game as a personal challenge. Anybody who was being promoted or depicted as a top guy in New York City, Jimmy always wanted to go head to head with him."

Tom Murray was our high school coach. He brought me up to the varsity as a sophomore. He was tough, but he cared about all of us. He taught us to value the basketball and to work to make our teammates better, not just ourselves. He's a legend at that school and has produced a lot of Division I-A players, including Jamal Mashburn, who would later star at Kentucky and go onto the NBA. And he never recruited players to Cardinal Hayes. Most of the private schools did at that time, but Coach Murray's philosophy was, "Just play with whatever kids walked through the door."

As Granda will tell you: "Coach Murray was tough to play for, but he taught life lessons that to this day that I catch myself quoting. 'Be on time. Be dedicated. Prioritize.' You don't know all that you're learning at the time. He was no nonsense and didn't favor anyone, no matter how much talent you had. For Jimmy, it was very good preparation for Dean Smith."

COACH SMITH'S FIRST VISIT

North Carolina recruited me fairly late. I do remember the first game that Coach Smith came to because my high school coach was tight. Oh, man, it was funny. That night we were playing at a high school that was only 10-15 minutes from my house. It just so happened that all of my buddies from home were at the game. So one time, close to halftime, we were going on a fast break, and I threw a fancy pass.

I actually thought it was a great pass— but my teammate didn't catch it and we turned it over. I was running toward the basket at the south end of the gym, which was the same direction of our locker room. Coach Murray jumped off the bench and told me to keep running right into the locker room. And he ran in right after me.

Coach Murray, who just finished his 38th year as the Cardinal Hayes basketball coach in 2006, remembered it this way recently: "I said, 'Keep going, James! Keep going right downstairs! I'm right behind you!' And then I yelled at him.

"But don't forget," Murray continued, "I had the support of James' mom for stuff like that. So I could do those sorts of things with him. And James could take it, too—he was one of those kids who was not only a good kid, but really tough. We wanted to make him really good."

Coach Murray, I never got a chance to thank you for that, so here it is: Thank you very much for your tremendous guidance and support.

At the time, though, I just couldn't believe how hot Coach Murray was after that pass. He would always get after me a little bit, but, that night, it was worse. He yelled at me awhile and then the whole team came running in a few minutes later because it was halftime. Let me tell you, I was thankful to see those jokers.

When we first got to the locker room, though, it was just Coach Murray and me. I was like, "What did I do?"

And he said, "Do you know who is here to see you tonight? Dean Smith!"

And this is the truth. I said: "Okay, Coach Smith—now where's he from again?"

You see, I didn't follow college basketball that much. And where we were, Dean Smith wasn't a big-name basketball coach. Lou Carnesecca was the big-name college coach in our world. I didn't really know who Dean Smith was, and at the moment, I could have cared less. I was there to play basketball. Of course, later on, that would all change.

GRAIG NETTLES AND THE YANKEES

You may wonder how I didn't know more about college basketball at that time or about Coach Smith. Let me put it this way.

My high school was one long block from Yankee Stadium— you could literally see Yankee Stadium from my high school. And I'm a Yankee fan to this day. We went to games on occasion, and we watched them all the time.

My favorite Yankee player of all time was Graig Nettles. Funny story—I actually had a chance to meet Nettles once. The Yankees came to Chapel Hill to play an exhibition game on March 26, 1981, just four days before we played Indiana in the national championship. I met Graig Nettles, and I told him he was my favorite baseball player. And you talk about making a youngster feel good? He said, "Man, you're my favorite basketball player!"

I loved the way Nettles played. Anything you hit over toward him at third base, he caught. The plays he made—I get excited just talking about them now. Some of them were frightening they were so good. He was a good hitter, too, especially in the clutch. (He had a couple of hits in that exhibition against our baseball team that day, too—the Yankees won, 6-2.)

I watched the New York Knicks, too—not just the Yankees. I can tell you about Walt 'Clyde' Frazier, Earl Monroe, Dave DeBusschere, Willis Reed, Phil Jackson, and on and on.

Muhammad Ali has also been a hero of mine for a long time, both for his athletic ability and his principles. When I was an assistant basketball coach at Notre Dame back in the early 1990s, we actually caught a shuttle flight from South Bend, Indiana, to Chicago together. We sat side by side and talked for 45 minutes— his wife was with him, and she helped the conversation along sometimes. When I got off that plane, I could have flown myself anywhere else I needed to go. That was an unbelievable day.

But getting back to college basketball—I seriously don't think I watched a full college game until I went to college. I just wasn't that into it.

THE VALVANO EFFECT

Well before Carolina ever got into the recruiting picture, I had pretty much decided that I was going to Iona. I was being recruited pretty heavily by all the local schools, and Jim Valvano was the head coach at Iona. I liked him. Pat Kennedy—who would later become a head coach himself—was the assistant coach, and I'd become very friendly with him, too. I liked St. John's a lot as well, being from New York City. But I had all but decided I was going to Iona. It was in New Rochelle, New York—only about 30 minutes away from my house.

In 1982, Coach Jim Valvano (right) was only a year away from winning an NCAA championship of his own at N.C. State. I came close to playing for Coach Valvano at Iona—he recruited me heavily—but happily made the decision to come to UNC instead. *(Photo by Hugh Morton)*

Then Carolina found out about me. I've been told two stories about how it happened over the years. Hugh Donohue, the former Tar Heel who played in the late 1950s and early '60s, told me that he had a brother who officiated games in our league. One of the stories I've heard is, Hugh Donohue's brother told Hugh that he better tell Carolina it needed to take a look at this kid in the New York Catholic League.

The other story I've heard was that Jim Valvano was somewhere where coaches gather and he told someone that he had the best point guard in New York City that nobody knew. Eddie Fogler heard that. Those two stories came together somehow, and they came to see me.

Coach Bill Guthridge actually came to see me first, then Coach Fogler. "My parents lived in Queens," remembered Coach Fogler. "I remember stopping at home, spending the night with my parents and then trying to get from Queens to the Bronx the next day. But I left my money on the dresser at my parents' home. I had to talk my way over the toll bridge, promising to pay double when I came back. So the first time I ever met Coach Murray, I introduced myself, told him why I was there, and then said, 'Can you loan me six bucks?'"

Coach Valvano was also recruiting my future roommate at Carolina, Chris Brust, at the time. Chris lived on Long Island. I was in the Bronx, so we didn't really know each other. But Chris remembers some of Coach Valvano's recruiting pitch to us back then, in the late 1970s, better than I do. "Coach Valvano told us he wanted it to be like CCNY back in the early 1950s," Chris explained, "when all these great New York kids stayed in New York and won championships." CCNY won both the NCAA and NIT titles in 1950, back when schools were allowed to play in both events.

Coach Valvano kept bemoaning the fact that the best New York kids were going elsewhere. Chris remembers Valvano telling him that he planned to stick around to build the Iona program, and he wanted to do it with New York kids.

Of course, in 1980, Valvano went to North Carolina State, and I played against him for Carolina six times in college. We were fortunate enough to win all six of those games. Chris said he saw Valvano once before one of those game and joked: "Hey, thanks for sticking around at Iona!"

Coach Valvano was always friendly to Chris and me, and I feel fortunate to have known the Valvano family for many years now.

THE PHONE CALL

I had a terrifying phone call to make several years before Coach Valvano and I ended up facing each other a half-dozen times in North Carolina.

My mother found out North Carolina wanted to recruit me, and we started talking about it. "Well, I'm really not interested," I said. "I'm going to Iona. I don't think I'm going to visit there."

"I think you should just go look at it," she insisted.

I obliged. I went to Chapel Hill in early April 1978, and got a chance to meet the players as well. I got down there and I was hanging out that weekend with Dudley Bradley and Al Wood. It was one of the most fun weekends that I'd ever had in my life. We went to parties. They showed me around town. We had wonderful meals all weekend. People don't realize that North Carolina has such really good people in its program. That's one of the beauties of it. And I rank Dudley Bradley and Al Wood as two of the top. If not for them, I probably would not have been at Carolina.

I came back home that Sunday night, and my eyes were as big as quarters. My mother knew. I said, "Mom, I think I'm going to go to North Carolina." And then I said, "Can you do me a favor? Can you call Coach Valvano for me?"

She looked me dead in the eye and said, "No sir, son—you're going to make that call yourself."

I waited for another two hours. I didn't have the courage to do it. But I did call—finally. And Jim being Jim, we talked a little bit and finally he said, "Good luck," but it was a tough call.

I told my high school coach the next day where I was going, and then I called down to Carolina and told them I was coming.

CULTURE SHOCK

You have to understand that when I got to Chapel Hill in the summer of 1978, I was still used to The Bronx. The first day I was there, I was walking on Franklin Street. A lady went by and said, "Hey! Good morning!"

That really threw me off. I looked around and wondered, "Who the heck was she talking to?"

We just didn't do things like that in The Bronx—I thought I had moved to another country!

I mean, I was on the train to high school in New York every morning, and I never got a "Good morning." In the train, it was all about individuals, all worried about getting to their destination and no one else.

My family brought me down to Chapel Hill. That included my grandmother Laura Freeman—my mother's mother—who's the love of my life. We all referred to her as "Nana."

To my family, that I was going to college was a big deal. Everyone in my family was buying these little trinkets for me: a clock radio, a black chest that had gold inlays to carry clothes, and other stuff. I think I was one of the first people in my extended family to go to college. Now that I look back on it, it was a wonderful accomplishment for all of us. But back then I really didn't think of it as a big thing.

They all stayed down in Chapel Hill for two days. And the toughest part was when they left. Then it hit me—Gosh almighty, I'm not going home! Let me tell you, I was a whole lot of homesick for a while.

THE SCRIMMAGES

North Carolina has always been well-known for the incredible scrimmages between current and former players. I got involved in those right away when I got to Chapel Hill. Phil Ford, Tom LaGarde, Walter Davis—a bunch of guys who were in the pros at that point—would all come back and play against us. Usually, we played in Woollen Gym; sometimes we'd be in Carmichael right next door.

That's when I first understood what a big deal Phil Ford was in Chapel Hill—he is the point guard that every point guard in North Carolina will be compared to, always. I got to hang out with him a little that summer and realized he was a great fellow. And it took me only about 30 minutes to realize that everyone in town knew him. As for playing against Phil, though—it didn't bother me to play against a legend. When I was guarding you, I didn't care who you were. Roll it out there, let's play. Phil was and is a legend to all of the people that follow North Carolina basketball. But on the basketball court, we were all extremely competitive.

LEARNING AS A FRESHMAN

Once our real practices started for my freshman year in 1978-79, I realized I had much to learn. I wasn't starting—Dave Colescott was the point guard—and I wasn't used to all the conditioning. We had to do a mile run. I'm a sprinter, and that mile run was the worst thing I've ever done in my life. It makes my stomach hurt even now to even hear somebody say the phrase, "Mile run."

Once, when I was a freshman, the coaches were running us to death. Just running us and running us, because we'd had a bad practice or something.

I said, "Hey, I didn't come to Carolina to run track. Why are we doing this? I came to play basketball!"

Why did I say that? There we went, running some more. That was a mistake.

Coach Smith had this rule that he enforced many times. When somebody messed up, the rest of the group ran, but the person who made the mistake wouldn't. That'll make you think twice about messing up. But we didn't have that much of that. We had a great group.

That freshman season was when I came to understand that Coach Smith was especially tough on his point guards. Because if you don't know the plays, how do you expect the rest of the guys to know it? So I studied the plays, and I ran when we had to run.

And I learned.

Going to college was a major adjustment for me academically, and then the basketball was on a whole different level. In high school, I could sometimes go through the motions and get away with it. In college, everybody's good. Take a play off, and you pay. I think the fans really missed Phil Ford. I think a lot of them probably wanted to send me home early in my career—and the coaching staff may have wanted to as well.

Fortunately for me, Chris Brust and I were roommates, and we formed a bond that year that will never be broken. That really helped. We talked about everything.

That team got upset in Raleigh in the first round of the 1979 NCAA tournament. We lost to Penn by a point on a day later known as "Black Sunday" in the state of North Carolina, because Duke also lost in Raleigh on the very same day.

TRAGEDY

I was a reserve again as a sophomore in 1979-80. I was playing a little better and understanding more about the "Carolina Way." But I had a very hard time during the second half of my sophomore season and then that summer as well.

My mother died in January 1980 at the age of 38. She had a congenital heart condition. She and I had always been very close. She was a wonderful woman, and even now I miss her. It's very hard for me to talk about her without getting emotional. (I love you, Mom.)

I know many people don't have good relationships with their mother and/or their father. I wish they would rectify that, because you don't always have nearly as much time as you think you do.

THE WRECK

All of 1980 was really a tough year for me after that. I probably wasn't a model citizen after my mom passed. One night in June, during summer school, I stayed up late at night. I planned to go down to the beach to visit a friend the next day. Several friends were over at Geff Crompton's house—a former Tar Heel who passed away in 2002.

Like a fool, I left Geff's house about 6:30 am. And instead of going to lay down in my dorm, I just went there, grabbed my bag, put some clothes in it and said, "I'll sleep when I get down to the beach."

I was riding with a friend of mine named M&M—we called him that because he told the ladies he was sweet. But M&M was sleeping by the time we got around Pittsboro. And so was I.

I dozed off, ran off the side of the road and ran right into a tree head-on. I didn't wake up until I hit the tree.

I woke up and said, "M&M, are you all right?"

"Yeah, I'm fine," M&M said, dazed. "Where are we?"

"We had a wreck," I said.

So we got out of the car. The first thing I was thinking about was I've got to get my bag out of the car. I don't know why I was thinking that—probably a combination of being very tired and being in shock. I went to the trunk and saw it was smashed in pretty good. And I got the bag. But I had to pry the trunk open to get it. Once I had it, for some reason I thought I was all right. Nothing was even in it except clothes.

CALLING WORTHY

A family that lived right across the street from where we had the wreck took us to their house and fed us a tremendous breakfast while we were waiting for the police to come. It was some more of that Southern hospitality that had so surprised me when I first came down from New York.

That was awfully kind of them, and I wish I knew that family's name to be able to express my gratitude once more. I don't, so let's just say, "Thank you again to that wonderful family in Pittsboro." Then the police came and we did the report. No ambulance, though—I didn't think I needed one. I just called over to Granville, looking for whatever teammates happened to be there, and I got James Worthy to come get me.

Here's how James remembered it in his interview for this book: "We had all been out earlier that night, having dinner, being college students. When Jimmy said he was going to take off for the beach, we said, 'No, no, that's crazy. Wait until the morning.' But we didn't actually stop him, and now I wish we did. We should have just taken his keys or something. I felt guilty about that for a long time afterward. He didn't really get very far before he fell asleep. The drive to pick him up only took about an hour."

James didn't need to feel guilty. I was the one who had made the decision. We were glad to see him when he came to get us, though. I had been walking around for at least an hour or so at that point. I thought I was fine. But when I leaned down to get into James' car, my back started killing me like you wouldn't believe.

James saw that. In the car, I kept saying, "Hurry up! Take me back to the dorm." And he said, "No way, man, no way. You're going to the hospital." We argued about that all the way to Chapel Hill.

I wanted to go to the dorm, and he wanted to take me to the hospital.

Fortunately, he was a lot bigger than me, and he was driving. I went to the hospital. I got to the hospital and suddenly everybody went into panic mode. I was like "What the heck is going on here?" People were running around and carrying on. Finally, a doctor came and told me I had chipped a couple of vertebrae in my neck. He told me I was very lucky—that if the injury had been in just a little different spot, that I could have been paralyzed the rest of my life.

'MAY NEVER WALK AGAIN'

So I had surgery, right away. They had to take a bone out of my hip to go into my neck. So I have a scar on both my hip and my neck from it. But I really didn't have any lasting effect from it other than that. I *really* want to thank Dr. Wolfe, his staff, and everyone at the UNC Hospitals who helped me during that time. I don't remember much about the surgery or right after that, of course. But I do remember that everyone there was so helpful to me.

And I do remember waking up. I was in the hospital room. I had a hospital gown on. It was interesting. I had to go through breathing therapy for awhile. And I had to walk very slowly at first. A few days after that, I was lying in bed and watching the local news. One of the local sportscasters came on, and he said, "UNC basketball player Jimmy Black may never walk again!"

I had just gotten up to go to the bathroom and come back to the bed.

I was like, "What are you talking about? I may not be walking very well, but I'm walking."

All that summer, after I got out of the hospital and was back in summer school and staying at Granville, I blared this song on my stereo. It was by Diana Ross and called "I'm Coming Out." It was my theme song that summer as I recovered from my injuries:

I'm coming out
I want the world to know
Got to let it show

I apologize right here and now to all of my neighbors in Granville who had to suffer through that song all summer long! But it was important to me at the time.

By the time my junior year had started—the 1980-81 season—I was ready to play again. I did have to wear a neck brace for close to six months after the accident, though, and my teammates kidded me about that. "We just killed Jimmy about that brace," James Worthy remembered. "It looked like the sort of thing a dog has to wear sometimes after it has surgery or something. He was probably doubly glad to get it off because of us."

4

1981

In many ways, the season in which we finished No. 2 set the table for the one in which we finished No. 1. In 1980-81, we came within an eyelash of the national championship. We lost four times as many games that season—eight compared to two the following year—but we made it to the NCAA title game both times.

As I wrote in the introduction to this book, when we got home from Philadelphia after losing, 63-50, to Indiana in the '81 NCAA final, our stomachs hurt. We never wanted to come that close and lose again.

But as I think back, I'm still very proud of that team. We had a great senior class that led us—Al Wood, Mike Pepper, Pete Budko, and Eric Kenny.

Al Wood paced our team in scoring for three straight seasons and scored 18.1 points per game as a senior. In his best game, he scored 39 points against Virginia in the Final Four to put us in the final against Indiana. Fans painted "Al Wood 39" all over Franklin Street in Carolina blue following that game.

Then, two days later, we lost the championship. I've still never seen the Indiana game on tape—I refuse to watch it. It just seemed like my teammates were throwing the ball back to me, and all of a sudden it gets in Isiah's hands and I'm chasing him. We couldn't stop him that day. It wasn't pretty, and it wasn't fun.

You see, everybody had counted us out in 1980-81. We had just lost Mike O'Koren, Dave Colescott, and Rich Yonakor. James

Worthy had been hurt for much of the year and he was just coming back from a broken ankle he suffered as a freshman—no one had any idea how dominant he would become. And Mike Pepper and I were going to be the guards, although neither one of us had played much. But people didn't realize we had been playing together for two years on the Blue team in practice. You talk about fun! After two years of that, Pep and I knew one another's game, and we were ready to roll.

We finished second to Virginia and Ralph Sampson in the 1980-81 regular season, losing to them twice, but won the '81 ACC tournament. We won both the semifinal (against Wake Forest, on a shot by Pepper) and the final (versus Maryland) by a single point. Then we took off for the West Regional, beating Pittsburgh, Utah on its home court in Salt Lake City, and then Kansas State to reach the Final Four.

Virginia, our old ACC rival, was waiting for us in the Final Four. But as Coach Dean Smith remembered: "Al Wood went crazy, and we also did a good job against Sampson." Sampson only scored 11 points—he had scored 32 against us in an earlier game that season.

The result was a 78-65 victory and a place in the final. The whole state of North Carolina was buzzing. Governor James Hunt bet that we would win, wagering a prize North Carolina hog against an Indiana hog supplied by Indiana's governor, Robert Orr.

The game would be played on March 30, 1981. It was a date that would become very well-known for far more than a basketball game. Indiana had blasted LSU by 18 points in the other semifinal. To top that off, Indiana coach Bobby Knight had deposited an abusive LSU fan in a garbage can following the game. For about 24 hours, that seemed to be a really big news story. Then we all understood that far more important things were at stake.

THE SHOOTING

The game was to be played at night at Philadelphia's Spectrum. Earlier that day, the president got shot. John Hinckley tried to assassinate President Ronald Reagan on the day of the biggest game of our lives at the time, which of course made the whole day surreal for everyone. For much of that day, we thought we weren't

An unhappy bench. This shot was taken toward the end of our 1981 NCAA final loss to Indiana, a team led by coach Bob Knight and point guard Isiah Thomas. That's me with my hands over my eyes. *(Photo by Sally Sather)*

going to play the game, and many of us didn't much feel like playing, either. This basketball game that seemed life-or-death to so many people obviously wasn't very important anymore.

There was some back-and-forth about whether our game should go on that night, postponed for a few days, or be played at all.

As Coach Smith recalled: "Before the game and after the assassination attempt on Reagan, we met with Indiana and the NCAA. Our chancellor, Chris Fordham, was with me. Indiana's chancellor was with Bobby Knight. Some of the top men from the NCAA were there, too. I joked with Bobby, 'Okay, let's just call it off. We'll just be co-champions.'"

Instead, once it was known that President Reagan's gunshot wounds weren't life-threatening, and his doctors had given a positive report as to his condition, we played the game as

CAROLINA
BASKETBALL 81-82

Check out the three-piece suits! In front of the famous campus landmark Old Well, myself, Jeb Barlow (middle) and Chris Brust (far right) posed for the cover of the 1981-82 UNC media guide. *(Photo courtesy of UNC)*

scheduled in Philadelphia. The president was still in a Washington, D.C., hospital, only 140 miles away. I was stunned at the power of television executives—that's still who I think dictated the decision.

But we played on. And under those strange circumstances, we played pretty well for a half. We led for most of the first half and trailed only 27-26 at halftime. It was a tightly fought contest. Even President Reagan seemed to refer to it in the midst of his crisis. When one of his nurses asked him how he felt that night, he borrowed an old line from comedian W.C. Fields and said: "All in all, I'd rather be in Philadelphia."

But Worthy got in foul trouble on some very, very questionable calls. Coach Smith had to bench him. And all of a sudden, Isiah Thomas really took over. He scored 19 of his 23 points in the second half. Worthy fouled out. I fouled out. Indiana won by 13. We all sat around looking stunned in the locker room after the loss. Sam Perkins just kept staring glumly at nothing. Matt Doherty remembers sitting in the locker room after the loss and talking to Al Wood.

"I'm a senior," Wood told Doherty softly. "I'm done. But you've got three more years of this. You've got to get this done!"

We finished 29-8 that season and No. 2 in all of America, but we hurt.

We had a team meeting in Granville Towers, where we all lived, after we got back to Chapel Hill. No coaches—they didn't suggest it, and they didn't know about it. We thanked the seniors for all they had done for us, and then we looked in each other's eyes and said this couldn't happen again.

It was a nice, warm day. We went outside and we talked about it some more. We were going to take a couple of days off and then get back to work. Because we couldn't stand that feeling again. It was second place, and it was terrible.

In the 1981-82 North Carolina media guide, all five of the freshmen were given equal space. While each returning player had a full page devoted to him, each freshman—John Brownlee, Warren Martin, Buzz Peterson, Lynwood Robinson and "Mike Jordan," as he was called then in the guide—received only one-third of a page each.

Coach Smith also had a tradition of always putting the seniors on the media guide cover. That's why Jeb Barlow, Chris Brust, and myself posed in front of the Old Well on UNC's campus in suits and ties for the cover.

The freshmen were listed in alphabetical order in the media guide, where they had given answers to a few questions to acquaint fans with their interests. Here were a couple of responses from Jordan on that long-ago questionnaire that he filled out in 1981—at age 18.

Question: Who's the athlete you most admire?

Answer: Walter Davis, Magic Johnson.

Question: What movies have you most enjoyed?

Answer: *Weapons of Death, Superman, Superman II.*

Question: What's the best book you've read?

Answer: *The Pearl.*

Question: What's your post-school ambition?

Answer: Professional basketball.

THE BOOTS

Even now, everyone remembers John Brownlee's boots.

John showed up on campus in the fall of 1981 wearing a pair of the most unique boots you've ever seen. Once you saw them, you couldn't forget them. I'm not saying you necessarily wanted to wear them—just that they were unforgettable.

John was from Texas, and his father was an executive with the company that made Justin Boots. So he had some serious boot connections.

"The boots were a Tar Heel-blue lizard skin," Brownlee recalled. "On the upper part, there was a Tar Heel symbol inlaid there. They were size 15 or 16—big ol' things. I still have them somewhere."

The boots had history. On John's signing day, Coach Smith had gone to Texas to witness the ceremony, and John wore the boots.

"I still have a funny picture of me pulling up my pants leg to show Coach Smith the boots," Brownlee said.

THE CONDITIONING

Our assistant coach, Roy Williams, was the tough guy for our preseason conditioning. Coach Williams had begun a more intense conditioning program for us before the 1980-81 season. "We had had some early losses in the previous years in the NCAA tournament," Coach Williams said, "and I thought we needed more stamina at the end of the year. I contacted Indiana and Kentucky, got their preseason conditioning programs, added some different things I got from our track coaches and made some things up myself. It was ridiculously hard. I made it very, very difficult for them."

It paid off, though. Says Buzz Peterson, 25 years later: "I always felt like we were trained to be in better shape at the end—in the final five minutes—than our opposition. Our minds weren't blurry then, they were sharp."

Of course, no one much liked the running at the exact moment we were doing it. "I've heard back from a bunch of guys over the years, and I know that they planned to kidnap me or beat me up," laughed Coach Williams, "but it never came through. Good thing for them—I could have identified them all. I'd have just told the campus police to round up all the 6-foot-10 guys on campus."

THE STARTERS

Coach Smith didn't choose the fifth starter until a couple of days before our opener against Kansas on November 28, 1981, in the Charlotte Coliseum.

He kept Michael in suspense. Michael didn't know for sure he was starting at one of our wing spots until Coach Smith wrote his name along with "Worthy, Perkins, Doherty, Black" on a Charlotte Coliseum chalkboard. We figured it would be Michael, though—Jimmy Braddock was more of a point guard who had a fine outside shot. Braddock would eventually take my place, starting at point guard alongside Jordan in 1982-83 after I graduated.

Coach Smith would say later that he made the decision before our opener in late '81 because, while Braddock was a good defender, Michael was a little quicker and at least four inches taller.

During the 1982 Final Four, the five starters gathered along with Coach Dean Smith for this formal shot. From left to right, that's Worthy, Jordan, Coach Smith, Perkins, me in the three-piece and Doherty. *(Photo by Hugh Morton)*

Kansas had a big guard named Tony Guy that Coach Smith wanted Michael to match up with and try to lock down.

"Michael really won the job with his defense," Coach Smith said. At the time, the start was notable. Phil Ford, James Worthy, and Mike O'Koren were the only three freshmen Coach Smith had started in season openers.

Braddock, then a junior, thought he had a decent chance at the starting job in the opening game, but, in his heart, he knew it wouldn't last long even if he did get it.

"I had a good preseason that year," Braddock explained. "Offensively, I was a good enough threat to start at the 'two' spot. And at the time, Michael couldn't shoot from the perimeter as well as I could. But defensively, it was going to be tough playing the other shooting guards in the ACC at 6-feet-1. For the first two to three weeks of the preseason, you could see Michael was trying to learn everything and was thinking a little too much. But once he got familiar with the system, he started performing a lot better in practice. It was just a matter of time before he started. Like all kids, I wanted to start every game. But realistically, you could already see we'd be a better team with him starting and me coming off the bench to back up both guard spots."

THE SEASON OPENER

That opener against Kansas was a high-profile game against Coach Smith's alma mater. The contest was televised on ESPN, still a fledgling sports network that had only been around for a couple of years. ESPN, in fact, was distributed so sporadically throughout the country at the time that Coach Smith couldn't get it at his own house in Chapel Hill. He mentioned several times during the season that he couldn't watch it at home. Hard to imagine that now.

Kansas had beaten us the year before, 56-55, in Kansas City. We entered the game with a No. 1 ranking by both The Associated Press and *Sports Illustrated*, but we knew it wouldn't be easy.

The Charlotte Observer said the day of the game about Jordan: "He comes to Chapel Hill billed as the next Al Wood, or another Walter Davis." So much anticipation surrounded Michael's debut, even though very few people outside our own team had seen him play yet.

Kansas was tough in that opener. We edged them, 74-67, after being tied at halftime. Worthy, beginning his incredible junior season, had 23 points and nine rebounds. Perkins went for 16 and nine. Michael, in his first game, had a modest debut—he hit five of his 10 shots and scored 12 points. Matt Doherty also scored 12. I just tried to get it to everyone in the right spots.

"It's good for us to have games like this," Worthy told reporters afterward in our locker room.

"I like playing tough teams," agreed Perkins. "We get to see what we're made of."

Kansas also gave us a preview of what we would see most of the season. Like everyone else, they were worried about Worthy and Perkins, and Kansas played us in a zone for all but the final three minutes.

THE REDEYE

Our three assistant coaches used to split up the scouting duties. At that time, it was legal for assistant coaches to go watch and scout opposing teams. Coach Williams recalled one of his strangest trips that season.

"This was one of my most ridiculous trips ever, and it just shows how warped my mind was in those days," said Coach Williams. "We were going to play Southern Cal early in the regular season, and Southern Cal was one of my teams to scout. So I flew to Los Angeles, checked into a seven-dollar hotel, changed clothes, and went for a five-mile jog.

"Then I went over to the exhibition game Southern Cal was playing that night and scouted it," Williams said. "I caught the redeye back late that night and was at our practice at 11 a.m. the next day. But I did that because I wanted to. I was the JV coach as well as a varsity assistant that season, so I had two practices a day and really didn't think anything of it."

We would win the Southern Cal game—the second on our schedule that season—73-62 in Greensboro.

TAKING A GOOD SHOT—PART 1

Since we were ranked No.1 for most of that season, right from the beginning, we were getting everyone's best shot. That made it doubly important that we took good shots from the field ourselves.

That was one of Coach Smith's trademarks. We would pass up the 18-foot open jumper to throw it to Perkins or Worthy inside, or to get a 14-foot open jumper a couple of quick passes later. In the first four games of that season—against Kansas, Southern Cal, Tulsa and South Florida—we shot 57, 55, 55, and 62 percent.

Not surprisingly, we won all four of those games by seven points or more, scoring in the 70s every time. Against Southern Cal, Perkins and Worthy each scored 18.

"Jimmy and I both understood that James, Michael and Sam would and should shoot more than us," said Matt Doherty 25 years later. "We accepted that. We knew that we'd have a better chance at capturing a ring that way."

Three current or former coaches of the Tar Heels as they looked in 1982: Bill Guthridge on the left, Dean Smith in the middle and a brown-haired Roy Williams on the right. *(Photo by Hugh Morton)*

And we were getting some good defense from our freshman. In that game, Jordan was matched up against a senior guard named Dwight Anderson, a 20 points-per-game scorer whom Michael held to a 7-for-20 night.

"He's a nice guy," Jordan told *The Charlotte Observer* after the game. "He talked to me a lot. And every now and then, he congratulated me on my defense. He'd say something like 'Way to cut me off from the middle. Good defense.' It made me feel good."

Jordan led us in scoring for the first time with 22 points in the December 3 Tulsa game, facing a Nolan Richardson team that had everyone back from its NIT championship the previous season. That was a good early win for us, too—we easily could have lost that one. I didn't play that well against Tulsa, bruising my right wrist and committing seven turnovers, but we were strong enough to overcome my off days, and that day was no different.

We played our first four games in the state of North Carolina—Kansas in Charlotte, Southern Cal in Greensboro, and Tulsa and South Florida in Chapel Hill. I had seven assists in each one of them, which wasn't difficult because I just kept throwing it inside and letting James and Sam finish.

Other head coaches, seeing the amount of talent on our squad, were deciding to zone us up and slow us down. In our fifth game, in Madison Square Garden against a Rutgers team that had just upset UCLA, we won a slower-paced game keyed by our defense, 59-36.

The team bus didn't show up for that one in New York for some reason. But Assistant Coach Bill Guthridge thought quickly and started flagging cabs. We piled into them in groups of three or four, with team manager David Daly handing out some petty cash to one player per cab and instructing us to tip 15 percent. That's how we got to the Garden.

TAKING A GOOD SHOT—PART 2

Winning games by scoring in the 50s—or, occasionally, even the 40s—became a fairly common thing for us as the season progressed. We would slow down a game, too, with variations of our Four Corners. We used it at some point in every game we played in the 1982 NCAA tournament, for instance. And we used it, with somewhat controversial success, in the 1982 ACC tournament final against Virginia.

There was no shot clock and no three-point shot in the 1981-82 college basketball season—although they were both on the horizon and would enter the college game for good later in the 1980s.

Because you could wait indefinitely for a shot in those days, though, we practiced "What's a Good Shot?" a lot.

Very seldom in a game did we ever take a bad shot—we took far more bad ones in practice. I can still hear Coach Smith now, stopping practice once after I had tried a long jumper with a man on me.

"My gosh," Coach Smith said, "Jimmy, do you think that was a good shot?"

"Yeah, I thought it was a good shot," I said. "I shot it, didn't I?"

(I've always been one for telling the truth, even if it wasn't the politically correct thing to do at the time.)

"Oh, really?" Coach Smith said. "How about all of you line up on that line over there and run for that 'good shot?'"

My teammates glared at me, and the running began.

Despite shooting 53.7 percent in the 1981-82 season, we would average only 66.7 points that year.

In Coach Smith's 36 years at North Carolina, the 1981-82 team was actually the lowest-scoring team he ever had. Amazing for a national championship team, isn't it? But we also held our opponents to 55.4 points per game—eight points less than any other team that Coach Smith ever had.

KENTUCKY

Our first really huge game of the '81-'82 season was against Kentucky. On December 26, 1981, when we met in East Rutherford, New Jersey. Kentucky was ranked No. 2 in the country and sported a 6-0 record. We were No. 1 and 5-0.

"My main concern," Coach Smith said before the game, "is whether we can rebound as aggressively as they do."

Coached by Joe B. Hall, Kentucky started Melvin Turpin, Dirk Minniefield, Derrick Hord, Charles Hurt, and Jim Master. All but Hurt averaged at least 12 points per game. The Wildcats didn't have center Sam Bowie for the game, however. One of the two players eventually taken ahead of Michael Jordan in the 1984 NBA draft (the other was Hakeem Olajuwon), Bowie had a broken bone in his foot at the time.

Bowie, at 7-feet-1, was second-team preseason All-America. Worthy made the first team, as did Virginia's Ralph Sampson, Houston's Rob Williams, and Georgetown's Sleepy Floyd—three other guys we would end up seeing often in March.

First, though, we had Kentucky the day after Christmas. It was thought to be quite a test.

And we passed it with flying colors. We beat them, 82-69—one of only three times all season we would pass the 80-point mark.

Worthy (26), Perkins (21), and Jordan (19) accounted for 66 of the points themselves. We held a three-point halftime lead and added more cushion early in the second half, keeping a fairly comfortable margin the rest of the way.

Like the 18,116 fans in attendance at the Meadowlands, Kentucky's players were impressed. "They may not want to say it, but they're still No. 1; and they're going to be there for awhile," Turpin said. "They're just great."

Said Minniefield of Perkins and Worthy: "They're the best inside combination I've ever seen."

And Coach Smith didn't have to worry about the rebounding—we ended up with a 37-25 edge.

THE GAMBLER

Al McGuire broadcast the North Carolina-Kentucky game for NBC—alongside Marv Albert, who did the play-by-play—and McGuire picked Kentucky to win it. This may have had something to do with the fact that McGuire and Kentucky Coach Joe B. Hall had become close. The two of them combined on a duet of Kenny Rogers' "The Gambler" for a record album called "Kentucky Calling Me" in the 1970s. Yes, I'm serious. It didn't sell a lot outside Kentucky, from what I'm told.

After the game, McGuire was singing a different tune. He said: "North Carolina is a lot more physical than Dean Smith's other teams."

WHAT'S MICHAEL GOT?

During that game, Kentucky tried so hard to concentrate on Perkins and Worthy inside that they left the rest of us with open shots.

"As for Michael, they just let him shoot anytime he wanted from outside," Coach Smith remembered.

Michael was 3 for 8 in the first half, and some of his misses were way off the mark. It got so bad that some people thought Michael should be benched for a few minutes, just to calm him down. A few days after we won the game, Phil Ford called Coach

Smith from the road. Phil was playing for the NBA's Kansas City Kings at the time.

"Phil told me, 'I got to wondering when you still had him in there after all those misses that maybe his high school coach had something on you!' Coach Smith recalled. "I think Phil's own father had used the line first, and Phil liked it."

Coach Smith got a big kick out of that. He still laughs when he retells the story. Michael made all five of his second-half shots and finished eight for 13 from the field.

A NEAR-HICCUP

We flew to California a couple of hours after the game. The cross-country flight was necessary because we were going out to play in the Cable Car Classic in Santa Clara, California, on December 28, 1981.

We played Penn State out there the very same day, and during the very same time that our football team, coached by Bill Dooley, faced off against a Lou Holtz-coached Arkansas team in the Gator Bowl. We had a good football team that year and ended up 10-2 after the 31-27 win over the Razorbacks. Kelvin Bryant and Ethan Horton were the offensive stars, each rushing for more than 140 yards in a game played in a dense fog.

That football/basketball combo caused some consternation in Chapel Hill, as people debated what to watch. At the Four Corners restaurant on Franklin Street, *The (Raleigh) News and Observer* reported that the restaurant manager was being offered bribes for the best tables in the house—the ones that had a good view of the two televisions showing the different games.

In California, we were lost in our own fog. With nine minutes gone, we trailed 13-3—the score really sounded like a football game. At halftime, we were down, 25-19.

"We were very flat in that game," Coach Guthridge remembered. "I think a lot of it had to do with coming off that big win against Kentucky and then flying cross-country."

Dick Harter, who later would become the first coach of the Charlotte Hornets, was coaching Penn State. The Nittany Lions were a very good defensive team and later would remind us of

James Madison, who would throw a massive scare into us a few months later in the NCAA tournament.

Perkins saved us with 23 points. He got us into overtime by scoring eight points in the final seven minutes, and I had a decent steal toward the end that helped change the momentum. Worthy had a rare off night offensively, going 1-for-9 from the field—his worst shooting performance of the season. And he fouled out with 5:20 left in regulation. But we still got it done, hitting our free throws at the end to survive.

"Maybe we needed a game like this just to shake them up," Coach Smith said right after the game.

The next night, we played the host team, Santa Clara, in the tournament final. We were thoroughly awake for that one and won by 19, even though Perkins missed the game with a sprained ankle. Chris Brust played well in relief of Sam, scoring nine points and getting four rebounds. For some reason, I was named the tournament MVP.

That finished off a fine start of the season for us. We would enter January and the meat of our schedule—14 ACC regular-season games—with a perfect 8-0 record and a No.1 ranking we were determined to preserve.

Following the Kentucky game, Perkins was asked if we could be beaten. With Coach Smith fidgeting beside him, hoping for a noncommittal answer, Perkins said: "At this time, I don't think so."

5

NAVIGATING THE ACC

In 1981-82, the ACC was very different than it is today. Although still an eight-team league, there was no Florida State, no Miami, no Virginia Tech, and no Boston College. There was no shot clock and no three-point line. You played everyone twice, at home and away, for a total of 14 regular-season conference games. You could drive almost everywhere, and frequently the road trips were 90 minutes or less. The league's geography has always been part of the reason why the ACC is so special.

As always, though, the ACC was a tough basketball conference. Following our 8-0 run in December of 1981, we would turn the calendar to 1982 and play 17 of our next 21 games against ACC opponents, including the '82 ACC tournament. While Virginia and Ralph Sampson remained our most high-profile rival, just as they had been the year before, nothing came easily to us.

North Carolina State, coached by Jim Valvano, was very good. Wake Forest was tough, too—the Deacons were actually picked second behind us in the annual preseason ACC media poll that season, with Virginia chosen third. Wake and State would later join us in the 1982 NCAA tournament—four of the eight ACC teams made the NCAA field that year.

And plenty of teams could be very good on any particular night. We almost lost North Carolina's famous home win streak against Clemson that season, and we narrowly escaped Maryland at home as well. Both Clemson and Maryland would end up in the NIT. Duke was in a down year—Mike Krzyzewski's second team in Durham would finish 10-17—but we still had some problems with them and also shared one strange afternoon with the Blue Devils when all the lights went out in Carmichael Auditorium on Senior Day.

As a conference, the ACC had quite a first quarter in 1982. Clemson, coached by 33-year-old Danny Ford, won the national football championship in the Orange Bowl with a 22-15 victory over Nebraska in January. Then, in basketball, our team and Virginia were ranked in the top three in the country for basically the entire season.

This chapter will take you through our next 10 games of the season from January until early February, including our two regular-season matchups against Virginia.

'THEY DESTROYED US'

We dispatched William and Mary, 64-40, for our ninth consecutive win in early January in a rare game at Carmichael that featured splotches of empty seats. The students weren't back from Christmas break yet. "The fans may not have been really motivated, but we were," Sam Perkins told reporters afterward.

Then we traveled to Maryland for our ACC opener on January 6, 1982. Perkins was motivated then, too—he was always motivated. Don't let the effortless way he played fool you. He worked hard. Sam led all scorers with 23 points as we beat Maryland, 66-50. Maryland coach Lefty Driesell said, as many coaches would that season, that the difference was Perkins and James Worthy.

"If I was drafting in the NBA," he said, "I'd pick 'em one and two. They destroyed us. ... This might be the best North Carolina team I've ever seen."

THE TOUGHEST TICKET

Coach Smith has seen the ebb and flow of North Carolina's many rivalries with schools in the ACC. In 1981-82, he will tell you it was no contest. Virginia was our top rival, and that was who we would play next. We would get them at home first, then travel to Charlottesville four weeks later. We were ranked No. 1 in the country. Virginia—making a mockery of that preseason media pick of No. 3 in the ACC—was No. 2 in America. The Cavaliers were 12-0. We were 10-0.

"No ticket that season was tougher than a Virginia-Carolina ticket," Coach Smith said. "That's what I always go by as who our biggest rival was in a particular season. In the 1960s, it was Duke-Carolina—it started that way because Vic Bubas had some good teams, and we had some, too. But then in the 1970s, our biggest rival was really NC State. The way you could tell was by our students' bumper stickers. You saw a lot more 'Beat State' on there than 'Beat Duke' or anyone else. And then Maryland had Len Elmore and all those guys, and they became a big rival for us for awhile. And Duke, once Mike [Krzyzewski] got it going in the mid-1980s, they became our biggest rival; and it's pretty much stayed that way ever since."

But in 1981-82?

"Had to be Virginia," Coach Smith said. "Of course, they had Sampson."

SAMPSON

During Sampson's aforementioned visit to Chapel Hill, I was one of his hosts, and we had a good time. Coach Smith thought he'd be impressed, and for a while, Ralph was. And after he told me that he was coming to UNC, I believed him. If he had, I think we could have won every game we played for four years. With all our talent, it wouldn't have been fair.

I remember when he told me he was coming to Carolina. It was a Sunday morning. After he said it, I told him, 'You recognize we're not going to lose a game when you come.' But then, next thing you know, he's a Virginia Cavalier.

So instead, he became a great rival for us. We ended up with Sam Perkins, and thank God for Sam. He always played so well against Ralph and tried so hard. Sam had those 41-inch sleeves—that's why he wore No. 41—which helped negate the huge height advantage that the 7-foot-4 Sampson had on absolutely everyone.

But you couldn't ever totally negate Sampson. He could handle the ball amazingly well for a guy over seven feet. "A freak," Matt Doherty remarked, "and I mean that as a compliment. Coach

Although Sam Perkins gave up nearly half a foot to Ralph Sampson, he played Sampson evenly for us so many times. Here, Sam is about to outleap Sampson for a jump ball. Sam says playing against Sampson always got him fired up. *(Photo by Sally Sather)*

Smith never really changed game plans for individual players—but he did for Sampson. We collapsed a lot more on him. We jammed inside and would try to make Virginia beat us from the outside every time we played him."

And Virginia wasn't just Sampson that season, either—they had a number of other fine players like Othell Wilson, Jeff Jones, and Craig Robinson, although they had lost Jeff Lamp and Lee Raker to graduation the previous year. All season long, we would battle.

THE FIRST VIRGINIA GAME

It was our second nationally televised, No. 1 versus No. 2 game in two weeks. We had handled Kentucky in the first one, but Virginia was a better team than Kentucky. We had everyone healthy, and we were playing at home. But Virginia had Sampson, and he was remarkable. He would score 30 points and grab 19 rebounds in the game—a dominating game for the first 35 minutes. Worthy was asked if he had ever seen such a performance after the game, and he said, "Nope."

But I was so proud of our guys. I fouled out with 7:23 left and Virginia ahead, 52-44. At that point, wrote A.J. Carr of *The (Raleigh) News and Observer*, "… the championship flags hanging from the Carmichael Auditorium ceiling seemed to droop to half-staff."

No one knew how much talent we had on our bench that season, though. We really did—it's just with Worthy, Perkins, and Michael Jordan on the team, you don't get to show it that much.

So in came Jimmy Braddock, who would play point guard in my place for the last 7:23. And Braddock was sensational. He swished a long jumper and then made four straight free throws late in the contest to help lead us on a great comeback and a 65-60 win. We made our last 10 free throws.

"I think we scored on about every possession down the stretch," Braddock said recently. "It's a very fond memory for me."

Virginia purposely fouled Braddock in the final moments, when we had a slight lead, and they needed to get the ball back. They thought he would be nervous at the line since he hadn't been playing much. Little did they know—that joker once hit 257 straight free throws in practice!

STATE AND DUKE

We didn't have much time to celebrate the win over Virginia. The following week we had games against two of our biggest rivals—NC State and Duke.

Coached by Valvano, North Carolina State was only a season away from its stunning run to the 1983 NCAA championship. The Wolfpack had Sidney Lowe, Thurl Bailey, Dereck Whittenburg, and Lorenzo Charles. They were ranked No. 12 in the country when we visited Raleigh to play them on January 13, 1982.

For awhile, it was close. The pace was slow, and we led 23-19 at halftime. Then, when we had a 33-32 lead in the second half, we started rolling, and State couldn't stay with us. Michael Jordan ended up with 20 points. "We lost our poise," Coach Valvano said right after the game. "Our mental game left us. When they went up 35-32, we started playing like we were 10 points down. We went into a frenzy."

We ended up winning, 61-41.

Three days later, we took another short road trip, to Duke's Cameron Indoor Stadium. Duke-Carolina is such a good rivalry that the teams' records don't matter. Duke led us at halftime, 32-31, and the Cameron Crazies were living up to their name. But having Worthy and Jordan on your side did matter. Michael had 19; Worthy had 17; and I ended up with 14 points and eight assists as we beat Duke, 73-63. Coach K got a technical in the second half, unsuccessfully trying to inspire his team.

DOHERTY AND THE CROWD

There was one unusual thing about that first State game. All that season, the State fans in Reynolds Coliseum would designate one player before the game to be a particular target of their hazing. They would yell at him or sarcastically clap wildly every time he touched the ball. Michael told a couple of newspaper reporters before the game he figured they would pick him, since he was a freshman, but instead they picked Matt.

Matt said later to some newspaper reporters that it didn't bother him. I didn't notice the whole thing myself—I always focused on the game and blocked out the crowd. But Worthy did.

"Matt was such a cerebral player," Worthy said in his interview for this book. "I knew he'd be a coach. He wasn't explosive, but he was so good at tendencies. If he knew someone liked to go left, he would overplay them so much they *had* to go right."

On occasion, Matt had a hard time with the crowd booing him. In that State game, Doherty was an atypical 1-for-6 from the field and 1-for-7 from the line.

THE FIRST LOSS

We were sailing along—13-0, first place in the ACC, first place in the country.

But life doesn't stay like that forever. The first real bump in our journey came on January 21, 1982, when Wake Forest came into Chapel Hill and upset us, 55-48.

Coach Carl Tacy used a zone against us, just as nearly every other team that season did. "But none of them were as good as Wake Forest's," Michael Jordan told reporters after the game. "That's the best zone we've seen all year."

Perkins missed the game, which hurt us. He was briefly hospitalized with a stomach virus and a 103-degree temperature. But that's not an excuse—give Wake Forest credit. That was a good Deacon team, led by their physical center, Jim Johnstone, who had 16 points and 10 rebounds that night. We led 22-9 after nine minutes, and then Coach Tacy switched to a 2-3 zone. We couldn't score consistently the rest of the night.

The 48 points rated as the lowest point total we had had since the opening of Carmichael Auditorium in 1965. That was embarrassing. No previous Coach Smith team had ever scored less than 50 in Carmichael before.

Coach Smith was asked a dumb question after the game—if he was relieved that we lost so that our win streak was over. "I'm *not* glad it's over," he said. "We want the regular-season championship, and this hurts that attempt."

Because of the loss, we would lose our No. 1 ranking as well. We dropped to No. 2, behind Missouri.

THE STREAK NEARLY ENDS

One of the most phenomenal streaks in college basketball is this—as of 2006, North Carolina had beaten Clemson 52 straight times in college basketball at Chapel Hill. Think about that—52 times in a row! And Clemson has had some good teams in those years, too. The streak started before I was born.

Well, that streak nearly got snapped in our championship season. Hardly anyone remembers this, but Clemson had a nine-point lead with nine minutes to go. We finally got going, but we didn't take our first lead until Doherty hit a 15-footer with three minutes left to put us up, 63-62.

Clemson sagged so dramatically on Perkins and Worthy in their zone defense that Matt and I were forced to shoot for much of the game. Both of us scored 21 points—career highs for each. We were lucky to escape. Then we beat Georgia Tech in Atlanta, 66-54, to set up a rematch with NC State at Chapel Hill.

SYNCHRONIZED DIVING

As a freshman, one thing we knew quickly about Michael Jordan was that he had the drive. You talk about a kid who went hard every day! By the time I was a senior, and I had figured out what I could and couldn't do. But here was this guy coming in every day just working his tail off—even after practice. Michael was special. He still is special. He got better every game. And the way he went after it rubbed off on everybody—even me, the senior.

I remember this one time when we were playing NC State in Carmichael Auditorium. It was January 30, 1982, and we were 15-1 at the time. We would end up winning the game, 58-44, but this happened while it was still very close.

There was this loose ball and Michael and myself, we both went diving for it. Just a straight-out dive, no regard for the body.

I don't even remember if we got the ball or not. But when I got up off the floor I thought, "Here's this young guy, and all of a sudden he's got me out here diving for a loose ball with him!"

I'm not going to say I knew right at that moment we would win the championship—I'm not going to tell you that lie—but I could tell you that I thought we had a chance to have something special here. I already knew about our other three starters and how good they were, and here we had another really terrific player, too, with a work ethic you had to admire. After that dive, that's when I knew for sure, "Oh, man ... we've got something good here—really good."

THE SECOND VIRGINIA GAME

We would have had to be really, really good to beat Virginia at its place. The Cavs were primed for us after that first loss and had won eight more games in a row since then. We went up to Charlottesville February 3, 1982, ranked No. 2 in the country, still behind Missouri. Virginia was No. 3.

And man, were they ever ready for us. I'm not sure anyone could have beaten Virginia that night at University Hall, a place where the Cavs had won 28 in a row. We weren't playing our best—far from it—but we had no excuses.

"They just played a super game," Worthy said immediately afterward.

Othell Wilson had 20 points and five assists for them. Sampson had 18 points and 12 rebounds. They beat us soundly—we never had the lead, trailed by 15 at halftime, and never made an extended run. Their fans loved it.

Once we finally got to within nine in the second half. But Sampson told reporters after the game: "It looked like they had used a burst of energy then. We went up by 13 then and they just died."

I said in the locker room the loss was "a slap in the face" to us. But I still wasn't sure that my teammates were taking it seriously enough. They weren't happy, but I wasn't sure they understood the gravity of the situation.

"We won the game," Sampson said. "And we're No. 1 in the ACC now. We'll just try to stay that way."

"This puts Virginia in the driver's seat," Coach Smith told reporters.

And where were the Tar Heels?

"In the backseat," the coach said. "Or riding shotgun."

THE TEAM MEETING

When we got back from Charlottesville, I called a team meeting in the room Chris Brust and I shared at Granville. (We didn't have a common lounge area, so most of the hanging out we did was just in one player's room or another.)

We just weren't playing well. After winning our first 13 games in a row, we had lost two of our last five. I can't tell you exactly what I said—25 years later, my memory of the team meeting we had following the championship loss to Indiana in 1981 is much more vivid. So I'm going to rely on some of my teammates for the details of the post-Virginia meeting.

"What Jimmy said was this: 'Guys, we've got to get more committed,'" said Jim Braddock. "'Every single one of us in here has to stop doing something that was hurting us. Maybe it's staying up too late … Maybe it's not going hard enough on every play in practice … but something. Everyone in here has to make one additional sacrifice.' And every one of us confessed to something we could improve upon. We all knew what our own weaknesses were better than anyone else, of course."

"I remember it very well," said Cecil Exum. "It was not what he said, but the way that he said it. Jimmy was very serious. I mean really serious—borderline desperate—with this being his senior year and all. This was it for him, and he wasn't going to let this one slip away. I believe the team wanted it just as bad. Jimmy could have a joke with the best of them, but we all knew that he was not joking."

"What I remember most about Jimmy's team meetings in general is that he would take charge so quickly in them," added Buzz Peterson. "If we had forgotten our roles, even for a second, he reminded us. The chemistry was unbelievable. We believed in our leader, Coach Smith, of course. But behind every team there is often a second great leader. We had two—Coach Smith and Jimmy Black."

6

RUSHING TO THE ACC TOURNAMENT

Gradually, we started playing better. This chapter will cover the 11 games we played from February 5, 1982, through the ACC tournament that ended March 7. In that ACC tourney final, we faced Virginia in a game that Woody Durham now considers to have had more impact on college basketball than any other game except for the 1966 NCAA final between Texas Western and Kentucky. Texas Western started five black players in that game. Kentucky started five white players. Texas Western's win, chronicled in the 2006 movie *Glory Road*, was a landmark.

Our ACC final against Virginia became a symbol, too, for different reasons. But to get there, for our third meeting against Ralph Sampson, our journey through the South continued.

A RARE DUNK

After the disappointing loss to Virginia, our first stop was Charlotte, where we opened the season with a victory over Kansas. We took a break from the ACC to play two overmatched teams from South Carolina—Furman and The Citadel. We had some fun in the Queen City—a place that would be good to us all season. Jimmy Braddock scored a career-high 16 points in the first game, when we romped past Furman, 96-69. That was easily our highest point total of the season.

Then, I actually had a dunk in our 21-point win over The Citadel. It was my first dunk in my four-year career at North

Carolina. Said James Worthy after the game, rating my dunk far more generously than it deserved: "I knew he could do it. I guess I'd give him about an eight on a scale of one to 10."

EIGHTY-TWO EXTRA SHOTS

Around this time in the season, Michael Jordan started staying after practice every day to shoot 82 extra shots.

That number was dreamed up by Coach Guthridge, who had done a similar thing for Walter Davis five years earlier. Although all of the coaches talked about our shooting mechanics with each other, Coach Guthridge was the one who instructed us. The coaches wanted just one voice to speak for the staff about shooting, so we wouldn't get too confused with too much different feedback.

"Walter was such a good shooter," Guthridge said, "but he went through a slump like all shooters do. So we came up with the idea of taking 77 extra shots after practice each day, since the year was 1977. With Walter, we did them purely from the baseline most of the time. A 10-foot baseline jumper is a hard shot, you know. Seems easy, but it's not. There's no backboard to work with, and you have a tendency to pull back a little and leave it short."

Michael's field-goal percentage was always pretty good as a freshman because he got free for so many shots near the basket. But around midseason, he was having trouble with his jumper. Coach Smith would point out many times that he thought Michael sometimes had problems getting the correct grip on the ball because his hands were so large. Coach said it would be like a normal person trying to get the right shot rotation on a volleyball.

Jordan had gone 1-for-6 in a game against NC State and 3-for-10 against The Citadel in a space of three games at midseason. So Coach Guthridge got him shooting the extra jumpers.

"With Michael, we didn't just stay on the baseline," Guthridge said. "We shot from all over the place. The key was for him to get some more confidence—and it seemed to work."

It did, gradually, although Jordan did express some frustration about his shot in February to Caulton Tudor of *The Raleigh Times*. "The defenses have changed on me. I went through a period when the other teams were giving me a jump shot against a zone," Jordan told him. "Right now, they are jumping all over me as soon as I touch the ball. I don't have as much time to get off shots. When I do shoot from the outside, I'm rushing it, and I know it. That's why so many of the shots are long."

The 82 shots a day must have helped. Michael ended up shooting 53.4 percent for the season, which is really good for a shooting guard. His career NBA percentage was a shade under 50 percent.

CAMPAIGN FOR A SHOT CLOCK

By the time we won a close rematch with Maryland—59-56 in Chapel Hill—it was mid-February. In that game, Maryland actually tried to hold the ball on us when the Terps had a one-point lead and five minutes left.

That went against Coach Lefty Driesell's normal philosophy—he preferred a running offense—but almost everyone had some sort of delay in their repertoire by then. Under the rules at the time, it was just smart basketball. If you had the lead, you wanted a game with fewer possessions and fewer chances to lose it.

Driesell had actually said earlier in the year, following another slowdown game in which Maryland lost: "Games like this are going to kill college basketball. I wouldn't pay two cents to see it."

So the shot-clock controversy was brewing already due to the many ACC scores in the 50s and even 40s that season, although the issue wouldn't come to a head for another few weeks in our ACC tournament final against Virginia. Ron Green, an esteemed columnist who worked for *The Charlotte News* at the time, wrote in early February: "I liked college basketball better the way it was, before the coaches started messing with it and wound up with some parts missing—namely about 40 or 50 points a game." Green went on to write that he had actually turned an ACC game off the other night because it was so boring and watched *Laverne and Shirley* instead.

Coach Jim Valvano was actively campaigning for a shot clock. "We're playing all these games with scores in the 40s and 50s, and it's no fun," he told the media that season after State won a 49-40 game over Georgia Tech. "The game is for four groups: the players, the coaches, the fans and the media. And I don't think any of them are having fun right now. Remember when the fans used to cheer when a team would hit 100 points? Maybe now they ought to total up both teams' points and scream when they combine for 100."

DOMINIQUE

We went out of the conference for the last time until the NCAA tournament on Valentine's Day, 1982, when we faced Georgia and Dominique Wilkins in Greensboro.

Wilkins had broken a lot of hearts when he left the state of North Carolina to play for Coach Hugh Durham in Georgia.

In 1979, Worthy (of Gastonia) and Wilkins (of Washington, North Carolina) were considered the best two high school players in the state. Three years later, their head-to-head duel was very even in our game. Each scored 19 points. Worthy added six steals—he was jumping into passing lanes long before most Tar Heel fans had heard of Fred Brown.

Dominique had a few great moments in the game, once jumping nearly to the roof to block one of Perkins' shots. Dominique already had his nickname "The Human Highlight Film" by then. But Worthy got a late steal and double-clutch layup to clinch a 66-57 win for us and set us up for our rematch with Wake Forest—this time in Greensboro, where the Deacons played some of their home games.

NO FIGHT SONGS

Chris Brust remembers that Coach Smith was annoyed by one thing in particular whenever we played at Wake Forest.

"Coach Smith did not like to hear the Wake Forest fight song," Chris remembered. "He would say to us in the locker room, 'Please, let's put this one away early and take them and their band out of it. I just don't want to hear that song tonight. I just can't do it!'"

That seemed like a hard task at Wake Forest, a solid team that had beaten us by seven points in Chapel Hill just a month earlier. But we accomplished it in style. Our zone defense worked very well and Worthy was again phenomenal, with 23 points and nine rebounds. "He's coming on like gangbusters," Coach Smith said of

Our home-game winning streak against Clemson came close to ending in 1981-82, but we managed to keep it alive with another fine win at Carmichael Auditorium. Little did we know that the streak would stay alive for 25 more years. *(Photo by Sally Sather)*

Worthy after the game. There weren't many fight songs this time around. We never trailed, shot 60 percent, and won, 69-51.

Late in the second half, we went once again to our "4-C" offense—basically the Four Corners. Wake Forest came out to try and guard us. Said Coach Smith in his interview for this book: "We liked when teams would play us hard in the 4-C, because that meant we'd shoot free throws or layups. That's what we did. Then the next game at Clemson, we had them by seven or eight points with about 10 minutes to play. We went to 4-C again, and they didn't do anything. They didn't chase us. I asked their coach Bill Foster afterward why they didn't, and he said, 'I didn't want to look like Wake Forest did and just watch a lay-up line.'"

WRONG-WAY GOZA

The Clemson game Coach Smith mentioned was down in South Carolina—we struggled with the Tigers again but won, 55-49. There was a six-minute stretch where we just held the ball outside without much protest from them. Finally, they started fouling us, and we made enough free throws to win.

Next up was Georgia Tech back in Carmichael. Coached by Bobby Cremins, Tech didn't have one of its strongest teams that season. They had a shooter named Brook Steppe, who was one of the leading scorers in the conference, but not too much else. Tech would finish in last place in the conference that season with a 3-11 record. We played Georgia Tech three times, and beat them by 12, 23, and 16. The most notable play in those three games came at the start of the second half in our game with Georgia Tech on February 24, 1982.

Lee Goza was Georgia Tech's physical center. He and Ralph Sampson had a couple of altercations, and Goza would even get Perkins riled up occasionally with his hard fouls. So we all had a laugh when Goza forgot which goal his team was protecting in the second half. He took the in-bounds pass, went full speed toward the wrong basket—and missed a dunk.

That was bad enough. If he had made the dunk, it would have been two points for us. But then Goza, still confused, got his own rebound and scored on a layup. That gave us the two points anyway. Goza was good-humored about it after the game. "I wish my mom could have seen that play," he said. "She always did want me to score for North Carolina."

SENIOR DAY

My last game in Carmichael Auditorium was February 27, 1982, against Duke. It was a strange, emotional day for several reasons.

We went into the last game of the season with an 11-2 ACC record, trailing Virginia's 12-1 mark in the conference. If Virginia beat Maryland as expected, we wouldn't be able to do better than No. 2. That would be our seeding for the ACC tournament. But Virginia lost to Maryland on a last-second shot by Maryland's freshman, Adrian Branch. That game was over well before ours was, which meant we needed to beat Duke for a tie for first place.

They introduced the seniors—Chris Brust, Jeb Barlow, and myself—before the game. It was definitely emotional. I cried on the court and wiped the tears away with my uniform. Then we started playing, with Chris and Jeb joining me in the starting lineup as is the Carolina tradition. Only 94 seconds into the game, there was a power failure. We found out later that a circuit near Teague dormitory on our campus malfunctioned. For an hour and 12 minutes, we had to go back to the locker room. We didn't know if the game was going to be restarted or not. We relaxed, ate oranges, and listened to music. Finally, the blackout ended. It hadn't been a total blackout—more like twilight, but too dark to play. Most of the fans stuck around—we've always had great fans. We rolled back on the court for a second warmup session. I think the delay had helped me regain my composure—we were playing extremely well as a team. By halftime, it was 42-17.

"It was an avalanche," Coach Krzyzewski said afterward.

The victory was a nice way to go out in Carmichael. Chris had 10 points and two dunks. It also meant we would have a drawing with Virginia at the ACC offices Monday to determine who got the No.1 seed for the tournament. Coach Guthridge represented our side, and he won the flip. So, officially, we won the regular season heading into Greensboro for the ACC tournament.

This picture was taken on Senior Day in 1982—a very emotional day for me.
A power outage shortly after our game with Duke began added to the day's
uniqueness. *(Photo by Sally Sather)*

THE EARLY ROUNDS

Our first two ACC tournament games weren't that easy, but the results weren't unexpected, either. We were commuting from Chapel Hill to the tournament in those days—it's only 50 miles to Greensboro—so each day, we got on the bus, played a game, and then rode back home.

The first round we had No. 8 seed Georgia Tech and beat them, 55-39. Michael Jordan had spent the previous four days in the infirmary with tonsillitis, but he got out just in time to play and led us with 18.

That same day—Friday, March 5, 1982—comedian John Belushi was found dead in Hollywood. He was 33.

On Saturday, we played NC State in the semifinals. State pushed us harder than they had in our first two meetings and was within four points with 1:21 left, but we made eight straight free throws. "I feel they beat you with defense," Coach Valvano said of our squad after that game. "They play the best defense of any team we've played."

Virginia won its first two tournament games, too, in nail-biters. That set up our Sunday final. Both of us had all but guaranteed No. 1 seeds in the NCAA tournament. But somebody was going to get to stay in the East, where Charlotte and Raleigh were two of the early-round sites. And someone was going to get shipped out—probably to the NCAA Mideast Regional, where that team would likely have to face a good Alabama-Birmingham team on its home court in Birmingham. We wanted to make sure that wasn't us.

THE LAST VIRGINIA GAME

We were back to No. 1 in the rankings by then. Virginia was No. 3. The game started on a Sunday afternoon—it had been moved from the old Saturday-night ACC final time slot to accommodate an NBC national telecast. And it started with a flourish. Virginia, assuming that Sampson would use his seven-inch height advantage over Perkins to win the tip, put both of its guards on the *offensive* end of the floor, trying to get a quick basket.

Perkins saw it, gathered himself and won the tip over Sampson. He tapped it toward Virginia's goal, where Worthy grabbed it on the bounce, took two huge steps and slammed home a dunk. The crowd erupted.

Perkins always got geared up to play against Sampson. "I always took it as a big challenge," he said. "I knew I'd be an underdog every time against him. I always tried to keep him busy when we played. I really looked forward to it."

Worthy got off to a thunderous start. After only 11 minutes, he had 16 points. Oddly enough, he wouldn't score the rest of the game. But he paced us to an early 24-12 lead.

Virginia was too good not to come back, though. Jordan picked up his third foul in the first half and had to sit awhile. At halftime, we led 34-31.

JORDAN'S BURST

Give Virginia credit. Virginia was playing without Othell Wilson, an all-conference guard who suffered a deep-thigh bruise in the first round of the tournament. But the Cavaliers were still good enough and deep enough to score the first six points of the second half to take a 37-34 lead. Coach Smith, who liked to save his timeouts for the last two minutes of the game, uncharacteristically took an early one.

Not long after that, Jordan got going—one of his most impressive shooting displays of the season. He had been missing early, but he kept getting open. "I still had my confidence," he said after the game. "I couldn't get my shot off like I wanted earlier, but the guys told me to keep trying to score."

We went to Michael four straight times. And he hit four straight jumpers for us—from the corner, from the wing, and twice from the top of the key. That gave us a 44-41 lead. Virginia scored to cut our lead to 44-43.

Coach Smith gave me the signal, holding up four fingers. On the court, with 7:30 to go in the game and a one-point lead, I called for the 4-C.

An on-court huddle, with me signaling to our bench and Michael Jordan looking on. I occasionally overruled play calls from the bench in favor of my favorite play—"Fist Four"—which meant I was going to throw it inside to James Worthy and let him work. *(Photo by Sally Sather)*

THE DELAY

Virginia had only one foul. To put us on the free-throw line, it would need to foul us six more times (in fact, this game still holds the record for *fewest* free throws ever attempted in an ACC tournament game—seven overall). But the Cavaliers didn't chase us. Virginia Coach Terry Holland wanted to keep Sampson back near the basket as a hockey goalie. We wanted him to come out on the floor, since we thought he couldn't guard Worthy or Perkins in space.

It was a stalemate. We basically threw the ball around on the outside for six minutes. The announcers for the game had a lot of free time on their hands.

The (Raleigh) News and Observer quoted Al McGuire, the former Marquette coach who was doing the game for NBC, screaming into his microphone once during the delay: "Pick up the tempo, guys, let's go. Let's have some action out there!"

Years later, our play-by-play radio man, Woody Durham still wonders exactly what Coach Holland was trying to do.

"Coach Smith always says about that game, 'It takes two to dance like that,'" Durham said. "Terry Holland honestly got out-coached in that game. He started fouling way too late."

It took Virginia nearly seven full minutes to foul us enough times to get us to the free throw line. Meanwhile, some of the fans in the Greensboro Coliseum chanted "BOR-ING! BOR-ING!" Both teams were booed with about two minutes to go during a timeout. We didn't care. We wanted to win.

Finally, with 28 seconds left, Matt Doherty got fouled and had to go to the line for a one-and-one. He made the first and missed the second—we were now ahead 45-43, but Virginia had the ball. We then used our fouls to disrupt Virginia. We fouled them twice before Virginia got anywhere close to the basket. Then, with about five seconds left, Virginia got the ball to its freshman forward, Jimmy Miller, in the left corner.

I was on him, and I wanted to be aggressive. I slapped at the ball and hit it. Miller claimed later I fouled him, but the referees and I saw it the same way. The ball glanced off Miller's leg and out of bounds—only the game's third turnover. It was our ball, with a two-point lead and three seconds left. Matt hit two more free throws, and Sampson had a meaningless dunk at the buzzer to make the final score 47-45, Carolina. James Worthy was MVP of the tournament, and we had captured the No. 1 seed in the NCAA East regional.

THE CONTROVERSY

We were just happy we had won the game. "I don't care if the score had been 2-0, it would have been a great win," Jordan said in the post-game locker room.

But many folks who had watched were unhappy about the delay that ate up a large part of the second half. We had scored only 13 points in the second half; Virginia had scored 14. Virginia's governor, Charles S. Robb, attended the game and griped to a Newport News (VA) newspaper as he left the arena: "You'd think the No. 1 team in the nation would have a little more confidence than to play slowdown with a team that has one of its stars sidelined."

The Raleigh Times said Coach Smith putting the brakes on the game had created "... a monster of a controversy."

Bob Quincy of *The Charlotte Observer* called the second half "... a test pattern." *The (Raleigh) News and Observer*'s Joe Tiede wrote: "The ACC could have provided an eye-popping show on national television instead of the most boring finish ever witnessed in its championship game."

Ron Green of *The Charlotte News* wrote: "Coach Dean Smith spoiled what could and should have been a memorable game when he reined in his horses that early. ... Calling off the last half of a game in order to insure victory is not my idea of giving joy to college athletes."

Sampson, interestingly, didn't rip our decision to milk the clock. "Each team has its own strategy, and you do anything that's legal under the rules," he told reporters.

It wasn't just us, incidentally. In seven ACC tournament games in 1982, only one team scored more than 60 points, and it only happened once. Coach Smith was irritated about the controversy. The day after the ACC final he gave a speech to the Charlotte Sportsman Club, where he said regarding the reaction: "I was shocked. They were saying the game wasn't a classic. But that's what the rules allow you to do. And if you're coaching a team and don't do it, me and every other coach in the country want to schedule you. ... The only people I need as a coach are the players. As long as they're behind me, that's all I want."

We were behind him. "It's not over yet!" I yelled in the locker room after we'd cut down the nets in Greensboro. Coach Smith had reminded the team of "Black Sunday" in 1979, my freshman year, when Duke and Carolina lost on the same day early in the tournament.

Still, we would get to play our first NCAA game in Charlotte, and our next two in Raleigh, if we kept winning. We wouldn't have to go out of state until the Final Four. That would help.

"It's good to have these games near home base, but we've got to put any idea of a home advantage out of our minds," said Jordan in our post-game locker room. "That's what Jimmy and Coach were warning us about."

THE AFTERMATH

The funny thing about Coach Smith was that he actually wanted to see a shot clock and a three-point shot in college basketball. He was way ahead of his time on that count. Since neither existed in 1982, though, he was just using the rules to our advantage. And that 1982 team would have been awfully good with the current-day rules, too.

Woody Durham believes the game was so significant because it galvanized opposition to the slowdown. "The game had an incredible impact on the sport," Woody says now. "I really think it was bigger than anything but the Texas Western-Kentucky 1966 final. It helped bring about the shot clock and the three-pointer. It made the game more exciting. And of course, Carolina would thrive under the new rules just as it did under the old."

Only two months later, in May 1982, the ACC would vote to experiment with a 30-second shot clock and a 19-foot three-point line. By 1986-87, the three-point line was a permanent part of college basketball, with the arc drawn at 19 feet, nine inches. The shot clock became a fixture—first at 45 seconds nationwide, now at 35 seconds.

Our game at Virginia was a watershed, but we didn't think of it that way. We were thinking of the national championship and what we had to do next to get there.

7

THE ROAD TO
NEW ORLEANS

o get to New Orleans, we needed to win three more games in
the state of North Carolina. The NCAA tournament was
different back then—smaller. As a No.1 seed, you got a first-
round bye, because the field was placed in a 48-team bracket
instead of the 65 today.

The bye wasn't necessarily a good thing. Coach Smith opposed
the idea, saying he would rather play a weak team in the first round
to get your feet wet. By the time you got to the second round and
started playing, your opponent had more confidence after a first-
round win. Nowadays, an NCAA team has to win six games to
capture the championship.

In 1982, the top seeds needed to win five. We would start that
quest back in Charlotte Coliseum, facing a James Madison team
about which average fans knew nothing. The Virginia school had
only been in Division I for six years. Most people thought James
Madison would lose in the first round in Charlotte to Ohio State,
a team led by rugged post player (and future television analyst)
Clark Kellogg.

But James Madison scored 14 straight points in the second half
to upset Ohio State and give us our first-round NCAA
opponent—one that, even today, is remembered bitterly as the
team that almost ruined our season.

JAMES MADISON

The Dukes were note a high-profile team. According to *The Charlotte Observer*, of James Madison's six top players, four had received but one Division I-A scholarship offer. But James Madison, well coached by Lou Campanelli, was a very patient team that didn't get rattled. The playing style reminded us of Penn State, which had nearly beaten us and did take us into overtime back in December.

We were favored by 15 points, though. On CBS, Brent Musburger said we should breeze into the next round. The fans in Charlotte certainly didn't expect a close game, but they got one. James Madison was the game that every championship team needs—a close, early call that you survive; something that makes you stronger. James Madison played us hard and well, with three different players scoring 12 points apiece. We missed nine of 16 free throws in the second half to keep it close. Although we maintained a four- to six-point lead much of the second half, we never could relax.

Finally, we got through, 52-50. "That game propelled us," Sam Perkins would say 25 years later. "We knew then for sure that every game would be tough—but that we were tough, too."

THE AUTOGRAPH

Before the game began, Kyle Campanelli—the 12-year-old son of James Madison's coach—came over to Coach Smith. He wanted an autograph, and Coach Smith gave him one. Smith also told Coach Campanelli before the game he figured it would go down to the wire.

"I thought he was just trying to be nice," Campanelli said afterward. "but I guess he really did believe we could play."

SOUNDTRACK OF THE SEASON

Whenever I think of music on road trips from that 1982 season and the NCAA tournament, I think of Lynwood Robinson. Lynwood could have been a deejay back then, and he's actually done some of that later in his life. He knew every song and every band. So Lynwood was the freshman in charge of the music—on the bus, or wherever we traveled, even in Granville if we were all together.

"I had to lug a big ol' radio around with a tape player in it," Robinson said. In fact, a reporter once described Lynwood's radio in print that season as "… only slightly smaller than a refrigerator."

So what was our soundtrack for 1982?

"Oh, I played Stevie Wonder a lot that year," Robinson said. "I remember I'd put on some Rolling Stones, because Matt Doherty liked that. The Who. Earth, Wind & Fire. I just kept that thing going on the bus, one song after another. No letup. It was a fun job, really—I got to set the mood."

SWEET HOME ALABAMA

We got no favors in the next round, either. Alabama had beaten Kentucky in the final of the Southeastern Conference tournament—in Lexington, Kentucky. With Coach Wimp Sanderson, the Crimson Tide was 24-6 and ranked No. 13 nationally. The game was played on a Friday night and carried live in North Carolina and Alabama—the 9:30 p.m. start meant that both *Dallas* and *Falcon Crest* had to be shown on tape-delay on CBS. For most of the rest of the country, we lost that television battle. Our game was the one that was tape-delayed—*Dallas* showed at its normal time.

Since the Raleigh regional was only 30 minutes away, we went to class all week. We did move into The Carolina Inn—the closest hotel to UNC's campus, both then and now—for a few days.

Alabama was a strong rebounding team, so we focused hard on that. The score was tied at 45 early in the second half, but then we pulled ahead by four at 59-55 and went into our delay. That successfully pulled Alabama out of its zone, and Perkins quickly fouled out Alabama's fine forward Eddie Phillips.

I had a tough defensive assignment in Ennis Whatley, a penetrating guard who would go on to a 10-year NBA career. I was fortunate; he wasn't hitting his shots—hitting just four of 13. All five of our starters scored in double figures. We were well-balanced that night and did what we needed to so that we could advance to the Final Eight against Villanova.

Matt Doherty drives inside in our NCAA tournament game against Alabama. This game was in Reynolds Coliseum in Raleigh—we didn't leave the state to play in the NCAA tournament that season until the Final Four. *(Photo by Hugh Morton)*

AN EARLY TIP

Our tip-off against Villanova was scheduled for 12:10 p.m., which caused some concern among the people who both wanted to go to church on Sunday and also to catch our entire game. A group of about 25 ministers in the Chapel Hill area petitioned for the UNC-Villanova game to be played and shown at 1 p.m. instead.

Reverend Robert E. Seymour was one of the movement's leaders and the pastor of Olin T. Binkley Memorial Baptist, which was Coach Smith's church. Rev. Binkley talked to CBS President James Rosenfield on the subject.

"He told me that CBS had locked into the schedule for over a year," Seymour said in a *Charlotte Observer* story. "But I told him that churches in North Carolina have had a prior claim on the 11 a.m. to noon slot on Sundays for the past 200 years."

CBS did not change the game time.

'THE NETS I WANT'

Villanova was only three years away from its own national championship, when Coach Rollie Massimino's squad would also face Georgetown in the 1985 final. Ed Pinckney—the post player who in three years would become the Final Four's Most Outstanding Player after Villanova's upset of Georgetown— was just a freshman in 1982. But the Wildcats already used him extensively, along with guard Stewart Granger and their talented center, John Pinone.

We were rolling along pretty well as a team by this point, however. Massimino had talked to his old assistant Lou Campanelli (now the James Madison head coach) several times on the phone that week, trying to get some recent scouting tips, but it didn't matter.

With a 28-22 halftime lead, Coach Smith urged us to get the ball inside more and force the action. In the second half, we hit 15 of 20 field-goal attempts. Pinone fouled out. Pinckney had 18 points, but Granger only had four. All five of our starters scored between 11 and 15 points, as we spread the ball around beautifully and won, 70-60.

The victory sent us to the Final Four. We cut down the nets in Raleigh, but one player didn't participate when it was his turn to use the scissors. That was Worthy, the Region's Most Outstanding Player.

Why?

"The nets I want are in New Orleans," James Worthy said.

A SURPRISE FINAL FOUR

So the field for the 1982 Final Four in New Orleans was set. Out of the 268 Division I-A basketball schools at that time, we were down to four teams. We would play Houston in one semifinal. Georgetown and Louisville would play in the other.

Surprisingly, Virginia didn't make it, and their loss to us in the ACC tournament final turned out to be huge. Because of that, the Cavaliers had to play Alabama-Birmingham in Birmingham, Alabama. UAB upset the Cavaliers, 68-66. It is now a rule that NCAA teams can't play on their home court during the tournament, but that was not the case in 1982. Ralph Sampson had 19 points and 21 rebounds, but Virginia badly missed Othell Wilson, who was limited to four minutes because of that thigh injury. Louisville then beat UAB to secure their Final Four spot.

The Charlotte Observer had held a contest to pick the four Final Four teams in 1982. Out of 2,427 entrants, not a single one got all four correct.

'SOOTHE YOUR THINKING'

Michael Jordan had a nice quote in the newspapers before the Final Four began. "I love to work with Jimmy Black. He knows what to run, what to call, and if you make mistakes he won't holler at you. He just tries to soothe your thinking."

UNC students, excited about our second straight Final Four appearance, applauded Michael and Chris when they entered their calculus class—giving them a standing ovation before we left for New Orleans.

By that time, Michael had been named the ACC Rookie of the Year. Worthy was third in the voting for The Associated Press player of the year, behind both Sampson and DePaul's Terry

Cummings. In my mind, though, it wasn't close— that season, James was the best player in college basketball.

SPITTING IN THE RIVER

Roy Williams was one of the most superstitious members of the team. In between JV games—which he coached—and varsity games, he didn't have much time to get something to eat, so sometimes he just grabbed a candy bar. A guy who was an usher at Carmichael gave Coach Williams a candy bar for a couple of games in a row early in the season, and we won those games. Then, on January 21, 1982, that usher wasn't there for our game against Wake Forest at home. Coach Williams didn't get his candy bar, and we lost. From then on, he always made sure to get a candy bar before every game, usually at a concession stand, and it had to be a Payday, a Zero, or a Fifth Avenue.

In New Orleans, though, he found out shortly before the game that the concession stands didn't sell candy bars. So Coach Williams talked his way out of the Superdome and back in just to go buy one.

And, while he was in New Orleans, Coach Williams heard it was good luck to spit in the Mississippi River. "I'm a jogger and I wanted some exercise, so the morning of the Houston game, I went jogging and spat in the river," Williams said. "I came back to the hotel lobby, and I told everyone there, including Matt Doherty's family, 'Well, I've done my part.'"

By the time of the championship game, Coach Williams had rubbed off on many people, including Matt's family—they were spitting in the river, too.

THE FIRST SUPERDOME GAME

The Superdome was enormous. The place ended up seating slightly more than 61,000 for both our games in the Final Four. Only a Harlem Globetrotters exhibition at an outdoor stadium in Berlin in 1951, when the Globetrotters played before 75,000, was supposed to have drawn a bigger crowd to a basketball game.

The 3,000 tickets that were furthest away were stamped "Distant Vision" and cost only $16. Those seats had to rely upon the large broadcast screens in the arena to distinguish between players.

They were so far away, though, that the players looked like ants and the only real view of the game was on the big TV screens in the arena. Wrote Ron Green of *The Charlotte News* about how far those seats were from the court: "Heck, I don't go that far on vacation."

The closest tickets were $36 apiece. The crowd seemed further away to many of us and, despite the huge number of people, quieter than it would be for a big ACC game.

Houston, coached by Guy Lewis, had a strong team. Clyde Drexler would become an NBA star, as would their sophomore center, Akeem Olajuwon. They also had a star All-America guard named Rob Williams, who was averaging 21 points per game.

Coach Smith put me on Williams. Again, I was fortunate. I just tried to make his shots tough, and he kept missing them. Williams went 0 for 8 and scored just two points.

Perkins, meanwhile, was having one of the best games of his career. He had 25 points and 10 rebounds, making nine of his 11 shots. We jumped to a 14-0 lead early but Houston came back—we only led at halftime, 31-29.

The play I most remember was this tremendous dunk that James Worthy had out of the Four Corners. He took off from foul line and absolutely *tomahawked* the ball through about three of Houston's players. To me, that was the game.

Curry Kirkpatrick of *Sports Illustrated* called it a "sledgehammer slam" and described it like this in the magazine: "Worthy spun around one Cougar at half court, flashed past another at the circle, took off from the foul line and didn't parachute to earth until he had drilled the ball through the floor. Dr. J, move over for Dr. James."

Olajuwon was not much of a factor. He got into foul trouble early and ended up with only two points in 20 minutes. We won, 68-63, to advance to the final. Georgetown beat Louisville, 50-46, in the other semifinal.

When James Worthy slammed the ball down for a dunk, the move was always ferocious. He wasn't looking for style points as much as he was looking to put a dent in the floor. Here, he dunks one over Houston in the 1982 NCAA Final Four semifinal. *(Photo by Hugh Morton)*

HOUSTON, WE HAVE A PROBLEM

Our victory over Houston to get into the NCAA final against Georgetown wasn't just reported throughout America—it was beamed into space as well. Two American astronauts from Houston were riding on the space shuttle Columbia at the time of the game and wanted to know the score, according to *The (Raleigh) News and Observer*.

The Mission communicator gave them the news shortly after the game ended. "I have some good news and some bad news," he said. "The bad news is North Carolina 68, Houston 63."

"Is that a final?" one astronaut asked.

"Affirmative," came back the reply.

Good news for us, though—we had almost reached our ultimate goal. Win or lose, my college career had only one game left.

8

GEORGETOWN

T he enormity of what we did in the 1982 championship game didn't register immediately with all of us. I knew we had won, of course, but I didn't know people would still care about that game and that season 25 years later. To explain, Michael Jordan knew he had hit the winning shot, but he really didn't understand the importance of that play at the time. After the game, he told a couple of reporters that the shot, in his mind, was only the *second-biggest* he had made at the end of a game. The biggest came, he said, when he played high school ball at Wilmington Laney.

"In high school, in the Christmas tournament, I made one from the corner with seven seconds left to beat Hanover," Jordan said.

The two biggest stars of the game—James Worthy and Patrick Ewing—had actually spent some time together before that Monday night. "I knew how good Patrick was. I actually helped to recruit him," recalled James. "He hit our campus, and he knew it wasn't for him. I don't think he had ever seen a southern campus before."

The game marked Coach Smith's fourth appearance in the NCAA title game—the first time he had been favored. Although he always downplayed the personal significance of a title, I had said a number of times once March began that we needed to win it for Coach Smith, to get that "no national title" monkey off his back. A lot of people had come to see him try and win it, too—his parents, who were both 85; his sister; his wife; a lot of his former players; and his former boss at North Carolina, Frank McGuire.

When you watch the tape of the game today, it's amazing how well it holds up. Some of the commercials seem very dated, though. Mazda advertises its new truck for $5,895. Atari promotes its new *Pac-Man* home video game.

But the basketball is full of sound and fury. Neither team leads by more than four points for the final 33 minutes. Coach John Thompson patrols the sideline in a cranberry-colored, double-breasted coat with his signature white towel draped on his right shoulder. Coach Smith instructs us calmly, sits for much of the game—including our last shot—and uses none of his timeouts (we still had four left when the clock read 0:00).

GOOD FRIENDS—PART 1

Coach Smith and Coach Thompson were close friends, which added another layer of intrigue to the matchup. Their friendship dated back more than 15 years, and Coach Thompson was Coach Smith's assistant on the gold medal-winning 1976 U.S. Olympic team.

They were both night owls and sometimes talked basketball late in the wee hours of the morning. "When the phone rang at one a.m., both of our wives knew who was on the other end of the line," Coach Smith recalled.

Before the game, Coach Smith said he had so much admiration for Thompson that he hoped that the Georgetown coach might be president someday. Thompson said he felt like a student who really wanted to beat his teacher.

After the game, incidentally, Coach Smith graciously said several times in his press conference that despite the win, he thought he had been "out-coached."

GOOD FRIENDS—PART 2

James Worthy and Sleepy Floyd—the two first-team All-Americans who would face off during the game—both grew up in Gastonia, North Carolina, which had about 50,000 residents at the time. Although they played for rival high schools, they were friends and had known each other for most of their lives.

"We used to go to church together at Tabernacle Baptist with the Floyd family," Worthy explained. "We knew the family well. He was a year ahead of me in school. He played at Hunter Huss; I played at Ashbrook. We dominated Sleepy's team, every year, up until his senior year. We had beaten them several times that season, but they beat us on a last-second shot in the 1977 4A state championship. The guy who ended up taking and making the shot for them—I would have thought Stevie Wonder had a better chance to make it than he did! But the guy made it, and so although I won championships in college and the NBA, I never won a high school state championship in North Carolina."

SAMPSON VS. EWING

It's funny to look back on what everyone thought about who was the best big man in the country before our game with Georgetown happened and the 7-foot, 220-pound Ewing opened so many eyes with his sensational game. Coach Smith told a reporter: "Sampson is a once-in-20-years type. Ewing may be in that category later, but people will compare him more to Bill Russell than anyone else. Sampson will have to be compared to Sampson. I don't know any big man who can run, jump, pass, and shoot like he does."

Of course, Ewing ended up having a far better pro career than Sampson. When you ask Coach Smith about Sampson now, he just smiles.

"Maybe one of his problems was he had too many moves as a post man," Coach Smith said. "You should just have one move you can count on and then a counter move. But he had so many, he didn't know which one to use."

GET IN YOUR SEATS

Cecil Exum, one of our valuable reserves, is a very superstitious guy. During the pre-game talk in the locker room in 1981, before the Carolina-Indiana championship game, Cecil told us we weren't in our regular spots inside the locker room and we needed to re-arrange ourselves.

"'Guys, we are not sitting in our usual seats, and I think that we should,'" Cecil remembered telling everyone. "I was a freshman, though, so no one listened."

One year later, Cecil made sure that mistake didn't happen again, and he got more cooperation. "They listened carefully the next year to me," Cecil said.

THE SHOPPING JORDANS

Michael Jordan and his dad, James, went shopping Monday to help pass the time. James Jordan saw 32 of our 34 games that season, and we all got to know him. He was a great guy, and it was a tragedy that he was murdered in North Carolina in 1993. The two were very close. Every year, all my former teammates notice, Michael looks more and more like his dad.

Anyway, the two Jordans went out shopping in New Orleans that day. "We talked a little about the game. He seemed looser than I was," James Jordan later recounted to *The Charlotte Observer.*

Michael said immediately afterward that he had visualized the game while shopping and later on the team bus. "I was thinking hard about the game," Jordan said. "I was thinking about how it might come down to a last-second shot, and I saw myself taking the shot and hitting it."

GOALTENDING: EWING

One of the things everyone remembers about the championship game was its electrifying beginning. That came about partly because Coach Thompson had told Ewing, his seven-foot freshman, not to worry about goaltending and to block anything he could reach.

Before the game ever started, Thompson had told reporters about Ewing: "Right away, he comes out and glares at you. He wants you to know that's his dominion, [to] stay away. He's not trying to intimidate. It's his competitive honesty. The kid is so up, so tuned in, so ready, so psyched."

Sam Perkins shoots over the outstretched arm of Patrick Ewing in our 1982 final. Ewing once took a visit to our campus during the recruiting process and, according to then-assistant coach Roy Williams, drank 18 glasses of orange juice in one sitting. *(Photo by Hugh Morton)*

He was ready, and so were we. Ewing—wearing his signature gray T-shirt under his Georgetown jersey to prevent catching colds—made the first basket of the game. It was an almost impossible baseline jumper that he literally shot over the corner of the backboard. Coach Smith nodded slightly when Ewing took the shot—it was the difficult sort of shot he wanted us to force—but it swished in anyway.

Then we started to run our offense, getting inside shots. Ewing tried to block everything. He goal-tended our first *four* baskets—two by Worthy, one by Perkins and one by Jordan.

We didn't care. We just kept pushing it inside. As Matt Doherty remembered: "They felt like they could intimidate us, but we'd been there before. We kind of huddled up on-court and said, 'Just keep throwing it to James. If they want to keep giving us two points at a time, that's fine.' They weren't going to intimidate us—heck, we'd played three games already that season against Ralph Sampson."

When Ewing left the game for a breather after about eight minutes, Matt scored our first basket that actually went through the net. His driving layup, on a feed from Jordan, cut Georgetown's early lead to 12-10.

Ewing would be called for goaltending five times—all within the game's first 12 minutes.

MY POINT (AND I DO HAVE ONE)

Chris Brust, my roommate and close friend, was the only one of our bench players to score in the NCAA title game. "That's my claim to fame," Chris remarked. "We won by one point, and I had the point! In fact, I had one of everything in that game—one point, one assist, one rebound, and one foul."

Chris also made the cover of *Sports Illustrated* the next week as well. His first minute of playing time in the game coincided with a massive Worthy rebound and slam-dunk follow in the first half that tied the game at 20. Chris was in the background of the picture, but his name and his No. 45 number were clearly visible.

Chris also gave us our first lead of the game. After Georgetown led or the game was tied for the first 15 minutes, Chris was fouled and made one of two free throws. That was his point. We had a

25-24 lead, and, at that point, Worthy had 16 of our 25–he was playing an amazing game.

EIGHTEEN GLASSES OF O.J.

The game would have looked very different if Ewing had decided to come to Chapel Hill. Coach Roy Williams supervised his recruiting visit and still remembers distinctly a breakfast he and Patrick shared at the Carolina Inn.

"We were going through the line, and Patrick picked up two little glasses of orange juice," Coach Williams remembered 25 years later. "The glasses were those really thin kind. I said, 'That's not going to be enough for you, Patrick. Go ahead—get as many orange juices as you want.' His eyes lit up, and he said, 'As many as I want? Okay.' And he proceeded to get 18 glasses of orange juice for breakfast, and he drank every one of them—every single one. I know it was 18, because they were all lined up on the table, and I counted them."

BUZZ VS. EWING

Buzz Peterson still laughs now about his role in the championship game—particularly one play. "I went 0-for-3 in that game," Peterson said. "I felt like it was tough to gauge my shot. But this one time, I caught the ball at halfcourt against Georgetown's press, and I had a lane to the basket. Patrick Ewing—who I had played against a little in high-school all-star games—was at halfcourt, too.

"So I think to myself: 'I'm going to use my speed and outrun him.' It seems like it took five minutes to get to the basket, but I was sure I had beaten him," continued Buzz. "But I hadn't—he was already there. So I took it at him and thought to myself: 'Well, there's no way he's going to block it. This ball is going up high! I throw it up to the height of the top of the glass; and you know what? He didn't block it. But it wasn't close to going in, either."

HALFTIME LAUGH TIME

Even in the heat of battle, Coach Smith and Coach Thompson found time to share one funny moment. At halftime, the two coaches and referee Hank Nichols got in a huddle.

Coach Smith said he had noticed that Ewing—who took so long to shoot his free throws that he flirted with the 10-second rule—had drawn the attention of the officials. If you held the ball for longer than 10 seconds at the foul line without shooting, you could get a technical, but it was a call you hardly ever saw. Ewing had a really long routine—he massaged the ball with both hands, dribbled, and paused before shooting.

Remembered Coach Smith 25 years later: "I told Hank, 'Please, no matter how much time Ewing is taking on his foul shots, don't call a technical."

"Hey!" protested Coach Thompson. "He's trying to set you up!"

"No, I'm not," Coach Smith said. "I could see you doing that, but not me."

Responded Thompson, while the official was still within earshot: "I don't mind if you don't call their pushing, either."

EWING AGAIN

It's hard to overstate the impact that Ewing, only a freshman at the time, had on the game. Although almost everyone remembers the goaltending calls, it's also important to note that Ewing had 23 points, 11 rebounds, three steals, and two blocks. He was everywhere—playing pressure defense 30 feet out on the court, swooping over the top for rebounds, hitting tough jumpers.

Early in the second half came just one example of why Ewing was one of the greatest opponents we faced that season. We led 35-34 when Ewing shot and missed … then tipped and missed … then grabbed the rebound and shot again, finally making it.

As Gary Bender described the action on television: "Ewing again. Ewing again! Ewing again!!"

Georgetown charged to a 36-35 lead.

A WORTHY DUNKFEST

Worthy's 28 points in the game included five dunks. James didn't really slam for style points—he slammed as if he were trying to dent the floor. Four of those dunks came in the second half, helping us take a slight lead.

Worthy was so incredible in transition, which is why Magic Johnson loved passing to him as much as I did. In the second half, he had two dunks on the fast break, got one on another rebound follow, and then one on a great pass that Doherty whipped to him for an easy two-handed jam.

The one against Sleepy Floyd, though, is the one that still gets played sometimes on NCAA highlight films today. We trailed 49-45 when Buzz Peterson stole the ball and pitched it ahead to Worthy. James had a one-on-one against Floyd, coming in from the right side. James took two dribbles, jumped and then held the ball high in his right hand. As Floyd jumped with him to try and block the dunk attempt, James slammed it through the goal.

The ball literally hit Floyd in the forehead after it burst through the net. Floyd also fouled James on the play. Worthy completed the three-point play with 11:41 left, pulling us to within 49-48. After that, neither team ever led by more than three points.

As Chris Brust said, "That was one of my favorite moments of the game—seeing James dunk on Sleepy Floyd's head."

JORDAN'S LAYUP

Worthy's fifth and final dunk, with 8:37 left, cut Georgetown's lead to 55-54. After that, we scored just two more field goals to go along with five free throws. Michael Jordan had both our buckets. And while his final shot is far more famous, his other basket had a higher degree of difficulty.

We were trying to extend our 59-58 lead with 3:30 left when Michael—standing near the spot where he would shoot "The Shot" a little later—got the ball and decided to drive. His quick first step, to the left, beat his man easily, but Ewing swooped over and gathered himself, ready to sky for another block.

Michael was already committed by this time—he was in the air with no teammate open, and he knew he had to shoot. So he

Before James Worthy and Fred Brown had a more famous encounter in the 1982 championship game, Brown had to watch Worthy dunk the ball right over him. *(Photo by Sally Sather)*

switched the ball to his left hand and put an arc on it so high it almost hit the top-left corner of the backboard. Ewing whiffed on the block because the ball was so high. But a ball shot with that crazy of an angle couldn't go in, could it? It could. The ball caromed perfectly, right through the net, and we led, 61-58.

Said Billy Packer on the CBS telecast: "Oh, what a layup! He put that ball up about 12 feet! Left hand!"

Agreed Gary Bender: "That was just amazing!"

Jordan—who, like Worthy, played his best game of the season against Georgetown, according to our coaching staff—would wind up scoring 12 of his 16 points in the second half. He also led us that night with nine rebounds.

THE FINAL MOMENTS

Ewing hit a 13-foot jumper for Georgetown to cut our lead to 61-60. Doherty went to the line for a one-and-one with 1:19 left, but missed the first one. Ewing got the rebound. Floyd got into the lane with a nice fake and shot a soft jumper that bounced three times on the rim and fell in to give Georgetown a 62-61 lead.

After we called timeout with 32 seconds remaining, I found Michael on a skip pass on the left side for his famous, 16-foot jumper that gave us the lead for good with 15 seconds remaining. As Michael would say in 2006, almost 25 years after taking that jumper: "That shot put me on the map in terms of how people viewed my skills on a national level."

Then, on Georgetown's last real chance at a good shot, Fred Brown panicked and accidentally threw the ball directly to Worthy. We won, 63-62.

In our locker room, we prayed together. Then, after Coach Smith talked for a few seconds, everyone went a little nuts.

"Once we finished celebrating, I felt like I had played two games," said Jimmy Braddock, "and I only played two minutes."

'TOTALLY DRAINED'

After cutting the nets and celebrating in our locker room, Coach Smith, Worthy, and I were taken into a nearby holding room in the bowels of the Superdome. There we waited for the

In the aftermath of our one-point win over Georgetown, we starters gathered for an on-court interview with the CBS announcing team of Gary Bender and Billy Packer. From left to right, that's Sam Perkins, behind Bender, followed by me (No. 21), Michael Jordan, Matt Doherty (No. 44), James Worthy, and Packer. *(Photo by Hugh Morton)*

Georgetown press conference to conclude so the media would have a chance to face us. The late Hugh Morton snapped a photo of our time in that room (we were joined by our sports information director, Rick Brewer). Mr. Morton, who owned Grandfather Mountain and turned it into one of our state's top tourist attractions, was also an extremely gifted photographer who took pictures of UNC sporting events for 60 years. He took many of the pictures in this book. He was also very close to Coach Smith. He saw us in that room and captured a moment in time with his camera—all of us looking totally drained and lost in our own thoughts.

If you didn't notice the nets still hanging from James Worthy's neck, you would have thought we had lost the game. I remember just feeling so spent. So exhausted. And, quietly, so happy.

Scott Fowler spoke with Hugh Morton about the picture a few months before Mr. Morton passed away from cancer in June 2006.

"That's my favorite picture I ever took that included Dean Smith," said Morton during that interview. "I think it shows a lot of things about him and that night. It's also important to point out that, while he's smoking a cigarette in this picture, he had the character and determination to give that up several years later."

"I told Hugh that he didn't have to catch me smoking like that," Smith said. "I've just taken a deep drag, it [appears]. I quit in 1988. Sometimes, when that photo runs in some publication or the other, the cigarette in my right hand is cut out of the frame. Sometimes you see it. I'm okay with it either way. That's the way

It looks like we lost, doesn't it? This is a few moments after our 63-62 victory over Georgetown, and it remains one of the most famous pictures from that night. Photographer Hugh Morton captured us all drained and alone in our thoughts in a stark cinderblock room at the Superdome, awaiting a press conference to talk about the victory. The only real clue that we won is the net draped around James Worthy's neck. *(Photo by Hugh Morton)*

After the Georgetown game ended, James Worthy and I answered questions from the media at the press conference. Worthy's performance in that game was amazing—28 points—but he did that sort of thing for us so often in 1981-82 it wasn't surprising at all. *(Photo by Hugh Morton)*

we all felt at that moment—drained, thoughtful. You can see it in our faces. It's a true representation."

Brewer is the only one in the picture who looks like he's very aware of the situation. He's checking his watch. "People see that picture even now and ask me why I was worried about the time after we just won the national championship," Brewer said. "What I'm worried about is East Coast deadlines. Our coach and our players haven't even spoken yet to reporters, and it's getting late. I'm hoping the Georgetown press conference ends soon. I want to make sure that all the newspaper folks are going to be able to talk to them before they have to go write their stories. That room was quiet—I remember that. Everyone was completely whipped."

Even some Tar Heel players who weren't in the room have admitted that photo has stuck with them for the past 25 years. "I've got a copy of it, and it's one of the best pictures I've seen in my life," said Jimmy Braddock. "You look at Dean's face, and it looks like he's thinking a million things. You don't look too closely, and you would think we had lost. It's an amazing photo."

'THANK YOU, JIMMY'

When we finally got to the press conference, I mentioned once again that Coach Smith had gotten the monkey off his back.

"It's a great way to go out," I said. "I don't think any of the seniors have gone out with a national championship, and I'm very happy about it. I'm happy for Coach most of all. Now I won't read any articles that you sportswriters will write that says he always chokes at the big game."

On the audiotape, you can hear Coach Smith say in the background: "Thank you, Jimmy."

A GLIMPSE OF 2005

Coach Roy Williams remembered the moments immediately after the Georgetown game very well. Williams, of course, was destined to win a national championship as the Tar Heels' head coach in 2005. A part-time coach that season, Williams worked fulltime hours despite his employment status and junior standing on the staff. Coach Smith, Williams has often remarked, worried far more about the financial fortunes of the Williams family in 1982, though, than did Roy.

After the Georgetown game, Williams had tears streaming down his face after the game and went to hug Smith. Smith told him, in a quote Williams has repeated many times since: "I don't think I'm a better coach now than I was two-and-a-half hours ago."

After the 2005 national final win over Illinois, Williams echoed his mentor, Coach Smith. "I don't think I'm a better coach than I was two-and-a-half hours ago," Coach Williams said.

FRANKLIN STREET

In our locker room right after the win, a couple of my teammates still remember me saying, "I wish I was on Franklin

Street right now." Traditionally, of course, Franklin Street is where everyone pours out to celebrate a big win.

Franklin Street went from ghost town to Times Square at New Year's Eve in about five minutes once the game was over. Police would later estimate about 30,000-40,000 people squeezed into a three-block radius of Franklin Street—partying and smearing blue paint on each other. One guy carried a sign that said, "If you love Carolina, kiss me (males exempt)."

Eventually, Chapel Hill and UNC officials hauled off five dump-truck loads full of trash from the scene. Buzz Peterson remembered that, for the next several years, people wearing gray "WG" t-shirts with Carolina blue paint spattered on them. "WG" stood for "Woollen Gym"—the t-shirts were standard issue for anyone taking a phys-ed class at Carolina.

"A WG shirt with blue paint on it meant you were there," Buzz esplained. "People wore those with pride for years."

MORE ON 'THE PASS'

In the Georgetown locker room, Brown answered the same questions over and over about the pass and how for once his peripheral vision had let him down. Everyone was impressed with his poise, some reporters so much so that they shook his hand following the interviews—a rarity.

Worthy, in our locker room, said he would always treasure that turnover. "To tell you the truth, the feel of that leather ball at that moment meant more to me than all the points I had scored," he said.

Coach Smith later said that he would have rather Georgetown not commit a turnover in the final seconds. His wish: Sleepy Floyd gets a pass from Brown, but misses the shot. "You hate to see a game end on a mistake like that," he said.

Fred Brown was and is a class guy. Thankfully, he would get his own national championship two years later. He was a senior when Georgetown beat Houston (and Akeem Olajuwon) in Seattle for the 1984 NCAA title. Coach Smith saw Brown after that game and congratulated him. Like me, Fred Brown would go out a champion in the final game of his college career.

CARLIN'S QUIP

In Charlotte, comedian George Carlin was performing in Ovens Auditorium the night of the game. The whole state really didn't close down for the game, you know—that's just a myth. According to *The Charlotte Observer*, Carlin announced North Carolina's victory and the score right after the game ended. Then, he made a joke at our delay game's expense.

"No one took a shot for the last 40 minutes," Carlin said of the game.

AT KENAN STADIUM

We flew home the next day. They held a pep rally for us at Kenan Stadium, and 25,000 people jammed into one side. We each had to speak for about a minute apiece. Coach Smith didn't attend—he thought pep rallies should be for the players. It was a pretty day, and he took one of his young daughters on a walk instead.

When James Worthy started to speak, the fans yelled, "One more year! One more year!" They wanted him to stay around for another season, but he wouldn't. How could you if you were going to be the No. 1 pick in the NBA draft?

Chris Brust pointed out his one point and joked to the crowd: "If I didn't make it, we'd all be in overtime in the Superdome right now."

Jim Braddock said UNC now stood for "University of National Champions."

During Sam Perkins' speech, he told the crowd: "It's going to be a good weekend. I just want you all to go crazy!" When the crowd roared its approval of this line, Sam quickly added: "Not that crazy!"

Michael spoke, too, and the crowd chanted: "Three more years! Three more years!"

"I'm just a freshman on the block," Michael said. "But I enjoyed my freshman year. I'll be here three more years, and I hope we win two or three more!"

He was there two more years, of course, but the Tar Heels never made it back to the Final Four. It's so difficult to do so. You need not only great talent, but a little bit of luck as well.

ON TOP OF THE BUS

After the pep rally was over, we all shared a moment that would probably never happen in today's world of safety belts and liability issues. We got back on our Trailways bus, headed from Kenan to Granville. It had to move very slowly because of the masses of people pouring out of the stadium.

Here we are atop the team bus following our return to Chapel Hill. Check out all the fans surrounding that Trailways—it had to go so slowly that being up there didn't seem dangerous at all. *(Photo courtesy of David Daly)*

There was a hatch in the middle of the bus that you could pop open and crawl out—I guess it was a safety thing, in case the bus turned over or something. Anyway, someone had the idea to pop it open and ride on top of the bus back to Granville. So we did, all of us. The team managers came up there, too. We had dropped off the coaches already, which was a good thing—they might not have let us do it.

It was a beautiful sunny day when we climbed on top of the bus. Sam has his long legs stretched out so far that he looks about eight feet tall. People were throwing us hats and t-shirts. It was great.

Said Jimmy Braddock: "That bus ride was the most unique and fun thing I've ever experienced."

"It was the best—we were kings," Cecil Exum said. "It felt like we were royalty, and I was in the middle of it all."

THE COMBINATION LOCK

Can you remember the combination on your locker in high school? Probably not. But James Worthy can remember the one on the door to North Carolina's locker room in Carmichael in 1982 because of its unusual symbolism.

"It's still hard for me to believe this, but it's true," Worthy recalled. "Coach Guthridge had to choose a combination for us to be able to get into the locker room if we ever needed to on our own, before someone else got there to open the door. He chose 32-2-1. And at the end of the season, we had a 32-2 record—and we were ranked No. 1."

1982 NCAA CHAMPIONSHIP GAME

NORTH CAROLINA 63 - GEORGETOWN 62

NORTH CAROLINA

	FG-A	FT-A	REB	A	PF	TP
Matt Doherty	1-3	2-3	3	1	0	4
James Worthy	13-17	2-7	4	0	3	28
Sam Perkins	3-7	4-6	7	1	2	10
Jimmy Black	1-4	2-2	3	7	2	4
Michael Jordan	7-13	2-2	9	2	2	16
Buzz Peterson	0-3	0-0	1	1	0	0
Jimmy Braddock	0-0	0-0	1	1	1	0
Chris Brust	0-0	1-2	0	1	1	1
Team Totals	25-47	13-22	30	14	11	63
	(.532)	(.591)				

GEORGETOWN

	FG-A	FT-A	REB	A	PF	TP
Eric Smith	6-8	2-2	3	5	5	14
Mike Hancock	0-2	0-0	0	0	1	0
Patrick Ewing	10-15	3-3	11	1	4	23
Fred Brown	1-2	2-2	2	5	4	4
Eric Floyd	9-17	0-0	3	5	2	18
Ed Spriggs	0-2	1-2	1	0	2	1
Anthony Jones	1-3	0-0	0	0	0	2
Bill Martin	0-2	0-0	0	0	1	0
Gene Smith	0-0	0-0	0	0	1	0
Team Totals	27-51	8-9	20	16	20	62
	(.529)	(.889)				

Turnovers: North Carolina 13, Georgetown 12.
Blocked Shots: North Carolina 1 (Perkins), Georgetown 2 (Ewing 2).

Georgetown	32	30	-	62
North Carolina	31	32	-	63

Officials: Dabrow, Dibbler, Nichols
Attendance: 61,612

9

AS OTHERS SAW IT

I don't care who gets the glory. Never did. I was into winning. I was never into interviews or publicity. Yet, Scott Fowler convinced me to include a chapter wherein some of my coaches and teammates recount their memories of me instead of always hearing what I know about them. So following are some stories about how others saw and experienced that title game and the 1981-82 championship season. There are some stories about how some of my teammates interacted with each other, too. The tales I like most in this chapter include the ones from and about my teammates who didn't get to play that much that season—they deserve more credit. But all of these stories come from everybody else's point of view, not mine.

THE GREATEST TEAM EVER?

ESPN Classic did something interesting in 2006 to try and determine the greatest college basketball team ever.

The channel put 64 of the best college basketball teams of all time in a fantasy bracket and seeded them. Then it asked fans to vote—either through text messaging or on ESPN.com—for the winner of each game. More than 1.25 million votes were cast, according to ESPN. The results of each game were broadcast live on a three-hour program on ESPN Classic on March 29, 2006.

The 1982 North Carolina team received a No. 3 seed, but America's basketball fans thought more of the squad than that. The team moved all the way into the Final Four, defeating the 1984 Georgetown title team (which won a title itself and sported a more mature Patrick Ewing) in the Elite Eight to get there.

In this fantasy Final Four, the '82 Tar Heels played the 1996 Kentucky squad in one semifinal, while the 1969 UCLA team faced the 1976 Indiana team in the other.

The Tar Heels received 54 percent of the vote against Kentucky to move into the fantasy final against the 1976 Indiana team— coached by Bob Knight and starring Scott May and Kent Benson. That Hoosier squad went 32-0 on its way to the championship. As of this writing, no Division I-A college team has duplicated that undefeated season since.

But fans thought that the '76 Hoosiers would have sustained their first loss ever if they had played the '82 Tar Heels. The 1982 Tar Heels got nearly 53 percent of the vote that night in the fantasy championship game, leading ESPN Classic and the voters to christen the 1982 UNC squad as "The Greatest College Basketball Team of All Time."

THE NON-SEVEN FOOTERS

Both Timo Makkonen and Warren Martin could have been listed at seven feet on the 1981-82 team. Instead, they were listed on every roster as either 6-11 or 6-11 1/2. This was a psychological ploy that Coach Smith used for years, although in the 1990s he finally relented and let Eric Montross and others be listed at 7-0 or above.

"Coach always told me he didn't want any seven-footers," Makkonen said. "His thought was that the other team will always play you harder if they think you have a seven-footer."

Makkonen and Martin had one of the closest friendships on the team. "Sometimes they called us 'the twins,'" remembered Martin, who was well known for his extensive comic-book collection. "I followed Timo around that year, really. It was neat. I never had a big brother, and that's what he became to me in college."

To the victor go the spoils: We all enjoyed cutting down the nets during our championship season. *(Photo by Sally Sather)*

PRAISE FOR A KID FROM NEW YORK

"Jimmy Black was the MVP of our 1982 team," proclaimed Matt Doherty 25 years later. "I know that's hard to believe given the talent we had, but point guard is the most important position on the floor. If you can't control the ball on offense and defense, you don't have a good team. I don't care how talented we were in the front line. Without Jimmy, we don't win that championship.

"Jimmy was a terrific defender and a very charismatic leader. People liked to be around him. When you in-bounded the ball to Jimmy, your concern was to get to your spot on floor. You knew the ball was safe.

"Jimmy was fun. He was New York, and he played to that. He was the guy who gave out the nicknames on the team. He was the one who was always coining phrases, who thought he was the best-dressed guy on the team. He made you laugh, and he was smart. You knew if he gave you advice, it was sound. You trusted him. You liked being around him. Good leaders include people rather than exclude them, and he did that. Black or white, star or sub, student or basketball player, he had friends in all different circles."

* * *

"Jimmy was a guy from New York, just like me. He was a cool cat. He was the guy on our team who was probably ahead of his time—he kept everything under control," said Sam Perkins. "On and off the court, he was always exactly the same guy. I always have liked him a great deal, and I really wish he had made it in the pros."

* * *

"What I remember most about the night after the Georgetown game is how me, Cecil Exum, and Jimmy Black walked the streets of New Orleans for hours, just talking. Jimmy kept saying how great his four years were at Carolina and telling me what I needed to do next year to become a better player. I think he was really relieved more than anything else," Lynwood Robinson remembered. "The thing Jimmy won't tell you about that NCAA tournament—because he's too modest—is he absolutely shut the other teams' guards down. Stewart Granger from Villanova, Rob Williams from Houston, Ennis Whatley from Alabama—Jimmy turned those guys off like you'd turn off a spigot. They got no water—not a drop. Defensively, he had a huge impact for us. You also need to understand what a leader Jimmy was. He was cocky, sure—you had to if you were going to survive in the world where he grew up. But he was a natural leader, and people gravitated to him. I believed whatever he said that year. Everybody did."

THE COVER OF *SI*

Michael Jordan has appeared on the cover of *Sports Illustrated* 49 times, more than anyone else in history. But he didn't make his first appearance on the magazine's cover for his entire freshman year with the Tar Heels.

Coach Smith declined to let Michael participate in a group shot of the rest of the team for the *SI* cover of the November 30, 1981 issue. Coach Smith said he hadn't decided on his fifth starter and so instead posed with James Worthy, Sam Perkins, Matt Doherty, and Jimmy Black for the cover. Coach Smith was diagramming a play in the posed picture as the four starters—without Michael— looked on. That cover shot is just about the only time you'll ever see Worthy without a beard. Coach Smith made an exception to his usual rule and allowed Worthy to have a beard because of a skin condition Worthy had, but Coach Smith asked him to shave for the *SI* cover.

Larry Keith, a UNC graduate and one of the magazine's lead editors at the time, tried to talk Coach Smith into relenting and letting Jordan into the shot, but to no avail.

Coach Smith later relayed that, until a few days before the team's opener against Kansas on November 28, 1981, he thought about starting Jimmy Braddock at shooting guard in front of Jordan.

"Larry had called way back in early October and said we want you on the cover with all your returning starters—and we want Jordan, too," Smith recalled. "I said, 'Have you seen him play? Because I haven't—not in a real practice, anyway. We hadn't even started practice. And I'm certainly not going to put a freshman in there when I'm not even sure he's going to start."

Ultimately, Jordan got the start—but not the cover. In fact, he didn't make a *Sports Illustrated* cover all season, even after his game-winning shot against Georgetown.

Carolina appeared for the second and third time on the magazine's cover during the NCAA tournament. First, "Tar Heels on a Tear" featured Sam Perkins on the cover of the March 29, 1982, issue. Then, after the Georgetown championship, *Sports Illustrated* used a picture of James Worthy dunking over Patrick Ewing in the NCAA final for its April 5, 1982, issue.

The headline: "Finally, it's Carolina."

Jordan wouldn't grace a *Sports Illustrated* cover until November 28, 1983, when he and Perkins shared one before Jordan's junior—and final—season at North Carolina. There would be 48 more Jordan covers to come (so far). Muhammad Ali, by comparison, has 39. Coach Smith has appeared on two—the 1981 cover and one in 1997, when he was named Sportsman of the Year.

THE PRESS CONFERENCE

In his interview for this book, Coach Dean Smith said he made a mistake in the postgame press conference shortly after the victory over Georgetown.

While describing the win over Georgetown, the coach took some time to criticize a story that had been published in 1979 in *The Charlotte Observer* as well as the story's author, Frank Barrows.

"I shouldn't have gone after Barrows at the press conference," Coach Smith said nearly 25 years later.

But at the time, the story had stuck in Coach Smith's craw—and he disputed its premise to an audience of sportswriters just after the biggest coaching victory of his life.

In November 1979, Barrows had written an exhaustively researched study of Smith's basketball program at North Carolina. At more than 120 column inches, it was one of the longest pieces of journalism ever published by *The Observer*.

Barrows said this in an e-mail interview: "The article I wrote was based on years of covering [Smith] and on 30-40 interviews, including two full days of talking with him in Chapel Hill. I even spent an afternoon with his parents, Alfred and Vesta Smith, in Topeka.

"The thesis that I evolved, through that research over the summer and fall of 1979, was that the life experiences that had shaped Smith had created a man singularly cut out to build, what we know now, would turn out to be among the finest runs of consistent excellence in the history of team sports," Barrows continued. "Yet, perhaps he was not always suited to taking maximum advantage of the superb individual talent he had on hand to reach for an occasional spike of greatness. This, of course, was long before the joke that Dean Smith was the only person who could hold Michael Jordan under 20 points."

Although Coach Smith respected Barrows as a writer, he was angry about the article's conclusions. "That [story] to me was so stupid, that your style of play means you could win a championship," Coach Smith would say in 2006. "Or you couldn't. That has nothing to do with it. You won ACC tournaments with it!"

Although Barrows covered ACC basketball for many years at the newspaper, he had stopped traveling by 1982 and had become an assistant sports editor by the time of the Georgetown-UNC game. So he wasn't in New Orleans. He was in Charlotte supervising *The Observer*'s coverage of the event.

Nevertheless, Coach Smith called Barrows out publicly in his postgame press conference, criticizing the 1979 story. Coach Smith's exact quote: "A bright writer in Charlotte once said the reason I hadn't won a national championship was because of my system. Now, I can finally say that's ridiculous."

"I thought it [the story] was so dumb," Smith asserted. "But I thought maybe some other writer would think that you had to play a certain way in a championship in order to be champions. Yet, there are a lot of ways to play. I said it kind of teasingly, but it came across more aimed at [Barrows] than it should have."

Barrows said in 2006 that Smith was always congenial to him even after his controversial story appeared, and that he didn't mind the North Carolina coach using that large platform to dispute the story.

"Journalists, many a remarkably thin-skinned lot, sometimes mistakenly believe that what they do is above criticism, or that their subjects are not entitled to fire back at them," Barrows said. "My perspective was, and is, this: I get to write what I think, and he gets to say what he thinks, and that's fair."

Barrows would eventually become *The Charlotte Observer*'s managing editor, a post he held for 13 years.

FROM THE NEWSPAPERS

Caulton Tudor of *The Raleigh Times* said this of UNC winning the national championship: "In the final five minutes—actually, the entire 40 minutes—it seemed the outcome of the game was riding on each play." He also wrote that UNC won the national championship despite the fact that it "… was as difficult as pulling the yellow out of mustard."

On the flight home from New Orleans, Chris Brust reads the New Orleans newspaper about our 1982 victory. Our plane landed at Raleigh-Durham, and then we went directly to Kenan Stadium for a pep rally that attracted 25,000 people. *(Photo by Hugh Morton)*

Ron Green of *The Charlotte News* called Black "… chloroform on defense and a stiletto on offense—a coach's dream at point guard."

Chip Alexander of *The (Raleigh) News and Observer* wrote of Black after one of North Carolina's wins over Duke: "And Black? The crafty senior with the smile of a choir boy and the hands of a Times Square pickpocket simply turned in one of his finest efforts ever."

Most North Carolina newspapers noted at some point during or after the NCAA tournament that Jimmy Black had set a new ACC record for wins. Black had appeared in 104 North Carolina wins at the end of his career. The previous ACC record had been held by Phil Ford.

THREE SHADES OF 'JAMES'

Of the top eight players in Carolina's rotation in 1981-82, three of them had the given name of "James." The players often used nicknames to differentiate the three—"Stick" for James Worthy; "Boss" for Jimmy Black; and "Daddy" for Jim Braddock. But the coaches didn't like to call players by their nicknames, generally.

Remembered Braddock: "The coaches said 'James' for Worthy, 'Jimmy' for Black, and they called me 'Jim.' It wasn't too confusing."

DIP, DIP, DIP

On the occasions when the players were on their own for meals, they were allowed meal money by the NCAA, and would generally receive $5 for breakfast, $10 for lunch, and $15 for dinner. David Daly, one of the team's head managers, would go to First Citizens bank on Franklin Street with a check from the athletic department the day before a game and cash it. He'd get lots of tens, fives and ones for easy distribution.

"I would keep the money in a blue First Citizens zippered bank bag which, of course, was always with me," he said. "After a road game, the players would make their way to the team bus. They usually sat near the back. Once everyone was in, I would stand and turn toward the back, at which point Jimmy Black would start the chant, 'Dip, dip, dip!' as I dipped into the bank bag to deliver each player their meal money for the night. Remember, we were all college students, and receiving money back then was a big deal."

FOREST AND TREES

"When I think back on that 1981-82 team, the first thing I remember is the level of talent," said Timo Makkonen, a redshirt freshman reserve in 1981-82. "I knew we were good but, retrospectively, I realize I didn't appreciate the talent. When you're in the forest, you don't see the forest for the trees. There was also a high level of camaraderie. We obviously had some conflicts, like you'll have in any locked-up life like that of a basketball team. But that was really a *team*.

"And Jimmy? He was the puppet master. He was the senior, the glue. He brought everyone together. We were a bunch of marbles running around loose, and he brought all the marbles into the circle.

"As for the championship game, you know what I remember most? Not Michael's shot, but the pass from Fred Brown to James Worthy. Michael's shot was magnificent in itself, and you were very happy for it, but somehow the pass, to me, was more memorable and more bizarre."

'NEVER LEAVE THIS PLACE'

From current North Carolina head coach Roy Williams, an assistant coach on the 1982 team, in his interview for this book: "My feeling when the Georgetown game was over with was more relief than joy. I kept thinking, 'They can't say negative things about Coach Smith anymore.'

"So," Coach Williams continued, "I wasn't jumping around. I had tears rolling down my face. Then we had the awards ceremony not long after that. And there wasn't a big stage like there is today for it. I remember Jimmy Black was sitting beside me as we waited our turn to go up there. And he put his arm around me and said, 'Coach, I hope you never leave this place. You're going to be good, but I hope you never, ever leave this place.'"

10

MATT'S MISSION

We never would have won the 1982 championship without Matt Doherty. He was a jack-of-all-trades for our team. He could pass, rebound, score, defend—whatever you needed. And he had a great feel for the game. As our teammate Sam Perkins says now about Matt as a player: "He could see it happening before it happened."

Matt has had such a high-profile career as a college basketball coach that some people have forgotten how good a player he was for us. But his teammates will never forget. Now he's the head coach at SMU, and I have no doubt he's going to be a tremendous success for the rest of his college-coaching career. He's a great coach. And he's always been so focused—a man on a mission.

As most college basketball fans know, Matt was hired at his alma mater, the University of North Carolina, in 2000. In his first season, the Tar Heels ascended to No.1 during the regular season. Matt was The Associated Press National Coach of the Year as the Tar Heels finished 26-7.

In his second season at Chapel Hill, the Tar Heels struggled. The team went 8-20. In his third season, UNC went 19-16 and missed the NCAA tournament for the second straight season. In 2003, Matt had to resign under pressure. I really wish it hadn't ended like that.

Obviously, there was a breakdown in communication somewhere in Chapel Hill. I'm not pointing fingers here, because I was not intimate with the program at the time. But to the powers that be—to the people who made the decision to get rid of Matt—I hope you're sleeping well.

And, to Matt: I wish you all the best as a coach. I know you will be incredibly successful for many years to come. And don't forget, Tar Heel fans, that Matt also deserves some credit for the 2005 national championship that North Carolina won under Coach Roy Williams. During Matt's tenure, the Tar Heels successfully recruited Sean May, Raymond Felton, and Rashad McCants—three starters on the title team.

For our 1981-82 title team, Matt was a sophomore starter and averaged 9.3 points per game. Originally from Long Island, he was our sixth man as a freshman, then became a full-time starter for us the next season and an important part of our journey to the national championship.

ADAPTABLE MATT

The coaches sometimes referred to Doherty among themselves as "Adaptable Matt" because he could adapt to whatever they asked him to do. Our teammates all knew that about Matt as well.

"Matt was Mr. Fundamentals," remembered James Worthy. "He did a little bit of everything. He'd say, 'I think I can pick up a charge on this guy,' after watching film. And, sure enough, he'd do it. He gave you the intangibles. And when you needed him to shoot, he could do that, too."

"When Matt came in as a freshman," said Jim Braddock, "I worried that he might become the backup point guard instead of myself because he could handle the ball so well. He was smart and a really good passer—just the ultimate team player, really. It got to the point where sometimes he didn't shoot as much as he should. And off the court, you had to respect him. He was a really good student and very organized. In college, he really was the clean-cut, All-American kid."

'THE BEST EVER'

As a longtime head coach, Matt has a unique perspective on that team from 25 years ago. When asked to name one of the things he admired most about Coach Dean Smith's handling of

Matt Doherty could do a little bit of everything for our '82 team. He was a great passer and sacrificed his own offense to get the ball inside to James Worthy and Sam Perkins. *(Photo by Sally Sather)*

our 1981-82 team, he pointed to the way Coach Smith put us in the Four Corners in the ACC tournament championship against Virginia, ultimately sealing that controversial victory.

"Coach Smith was the best ever at utilizing the rules to his team's benefit," said Doherty. "The rules stated we could hold the ball. They had a guy in Ralph Sampson who was 7-foot-4 and camped under the basket. We didn't think he could guard Perkins or Worthy 20 feet from the basket.

"People really should be mad at Virginia for not forcing the action, not us," Doherty continued. "And I don't care what rules you played with that '82 team. When you had Worthy, Perkins and Michael, you could have played the old girls' high school rules, where it's six-on-six, and you can't cross half-court because you only have three on offense and three on defense. Wouldn't have mattered—that team would have been good doing anything."

A VIEW OF "THE SHOT"

Matt also had a fine perspective on Michael Jordan's shot that beat Georgetown. Only Matt, myself, and Jordan touched the ball on that final possession, and Matt says, to this day, he still thinks about Michael's shot and smiles.

Michael Jordan and Matt Doherty wait at the scorer's table to check into a game. *(Photo by Hugh Morton)*

"I remember it well," Doherty said. "We called that timeout, and Coach Smith spoke with great confidence. In those situations, he always had a way of making you feel comfortable—of making everybody in the huddle feel like they could make the last shot. That's a special gift he has; so we were confident going out there that we were in pretty good shape. They came out in a zone and we swung the ball. I was at the foul line and had it for a few seconds, but not for long. I tell you, it still blows my mind today that Michael took that shot. He's a freshman—*a freshman!*—in front of 60,000 people and a national-television audience. There was still plenty of time when he caught the ball. He could have faked the shot and passed it, and no one would have said he's afraid to shoot. He was open, yes, but it wasn't as if somebody fell down. He wasn't *that* open.

"But for a freshman to get the ball and shoot it in that situation like he was shooting in a shooting drill, to me is still one of the most fascinating things I've ever seen. I've got a picture of that shot in my office. It still blows my mind, seriously, that Michael had that sort of composure. If it's three seconds, sure, he has to shoot it, but not with 17 seconds left. He doesn't have to, but he does—and then the ball just goes in the heart of the goal."

COMING THROUGH

Coach Dean Smith remembers Matt as one of those players who got it done when he needed to and no matter where the coaches placed him on the floor.

"On that 1982 team, our '2' and '3' positions were really interchangeable," Smith said, smiling. "We did the same sorts of things with both Matt and Michael Jordan with one exception—we ran the backdoor play for Michael for the dunk a lot more often than we ever did for Matt."

Matt played many big games for us that season. Some of them were even in the scoring column, although, like me, he preferred to pass. But Matt had 18 points in a win over Tulsa, 18 more in a victory over Maryland and 21 against Clemson.

Smith recalled one game in particular in the NCAA tournament as Doherty's best of the season.

"When we played Alabama, they really decided to give him shots," Smith said. "And he made them. He came through for us."

STAND OUT IN STYLE

Before Matt got into coaching and after his playing career, he was a bond trader for three-plus years on Wall Street. He got tired of that, though, quit that job, and moved to Charlotte. He did a little television work as a color commentator, but he also had a dream of opening a sleek clothing store for big men. This was the late 1980s, and the Charlotte Hornets had just entered the NBA. Matt figured he could cater to all the visiting NBA teams that came into town to play the Hornets. Knowing how smart he is, he could have figured out a way.

He even had a name for his proposed store. He planned to call it "Stand Out In Style," he has told reporters on several occasions.

The store never was built, though. Before Matt got too serious about the idea, Davidson head basketball coach Bob McKillop hired him as an assistant in 1989. From there, Matt moved to Kansas in 1992 to work for Roy Williams as an assistant, and he stayed in Kansas until Notre Dame hired him as its head coach in 1999.

After one season at Notre Dame, Matt replaced Coach Guthridge, who was retiring, as the head coach at North Carolina in 2000. After his Tar Heel job ended in 2003, he stayed out of coaching for two seasons and worked as a television analyst. Matt then returned at Florida Atlantic University in Boca Raton, Florida, in 2005. After one successful season there, SMU hired him in 2006, and he plans to be there awhile.

"I view this as a destination job," Matt said when he was introduced on the SMU campus in Dallas.

INVOKING '82

Wherever he has been as a college head coach—Notre Dame, North Carolina, Florida Atlantic and now SMU—Doherty has reminisced with his players about 1982 and our championship season and tried to get them to learn from it.

"Whenever I think of 1982, I smile," Doherty said. "It was a proud year for everyone involved. The coming together of individuals for a common goal—there's not many more things in life more rewarding than that."

11

ARE THEY WORTHY?

J ames Worthy, as I've stated before, was the best player in college basketball in 1981-82, without question. With the L.A. Lakers and their "Showtime" fast break, James, a hall of famer, was an integral part of three NBA championship teams (in 1985, '87 and '88).

As he did for us in 1982, he always lived up to his "Big Game James" nickname with the Lakers under coach Pat Riley. He averaged 17.6 points per game throughout his regular-season career, but upped that to 21.1 points per game in the postseason. As Magic Johnson said at the news conference the Lakers held when James retired from the NBA in 1994, James was one of the best five "playoff players" in NBA history. The NBA also named James as one of its 50 greatest players ever during the 1990s.

We, of course, were lucky to have him first. I feel so fortunate I got to throw the ball down to James when the going got tough.

Like the rest of us on that team, James really didn't care who got the credit. He averaged 15.6 points per game on our 1982 team. He could have averaged 25 if he had been a selfish player. But he never was one. In the NBA, he also had very well known teammates—Magic was in L.A. then, as well as Kareem Abdul-Jabbar. James never had a problem with that.

But James says that his association with our 1982 team follows him around even now, 25 years later. In 2006, he recalled with a laugh: "I was MVP of the Final Four. I scored 28 points against Georgetown. And every time I walk through the airport now, someone says to me, 'Hey, wait a minute, I know you. You're, you're … I know! Aren't you the guy who used to play with Michael Jordan in college?"

Since 1982, Worthy has made the West Coast his permanent home. He's doing very well out there now, more than 10 years after his retirement from basketball.

At age 45, James is single and the father of two teenaged daughters, who play basketball and soccer. He lives near the UCLA campus and does a lot of television work in L.A., mostly on the Lakers' television broadcasts—so he sees a lot of Kobe Bryant. He also hosts a local half-hour sports show and has started to become something of a business entrepreneur.

This chapter contains stories told by James and others about his great career at Chapel Hill—one that would ultimately end with his No. 52 becoming one of the six retired numbers in Carolina basketball history. Only Lennie Rosenbluth, Phil Ford, George Glamack, Antawn Jamison, and Michael Jordan share that honor.

ONE-ON-ONE WITH MJ

Occasionally, after practice, some of us would stick around and play one-on-one with each other. Jordan and Worthy didn't face off very often that 1981-82 season, but they did a few times.

"We would play one-on-one to five that season, with each basket counting a single point," James explained. "Michael and I played three games that year—he always wanted to play me, but I didn't really care to do it that often. I won two of the three times that we played. So I beat him, 2-1! And that was it. I wouldn't play him anymore. So I'm still up, 2-1, in our career series. He still bugs me about that whenever I see him. He still wants revenge."

CHARLIE SCOTT CONNECTION

Gastonia, North Carolina, where James grew up, is only about a two-and-a-half-hour drive to Chapel Hill. So Coach Smith and his staff had a geographical advantage in recruiting James. But it wasn't just that.

As James recalled: "My parents knew all about Charlie Scott. They knew he was the first black player to come to North

Carolina, how well he did, and how Coach Smith had treated him with such respect. My mom and dad just thought so highly of Coach Smith because of that. As for me, I started going to basketball camp up there in eighth grade. I was really in love with Phil Ford back then—he was my idol. I kind of knew that was where my heart was all through the recruiting process."

James' parents—Ervin and Gladys Worthy—who are both now deceased, were great people. They were around us a lot that season, including at the Final Four.

A 'HARDSHIP' CASE

Coach Smith said that James was the best high school basketball player he had ever seen. Back in those more innocent days of recruiting, most of us didn't get much interest until we were high school juniors or seniors. But James was literally on the Carolina radar screen since that eighth-grade basketball camp.

"If he had been able to go hardship out of high school, we would have started him here as a 10th-grader," Coach Smith said. "I'm serious. We kept having to move him up to play against older players in the basketball camps; he was way too good for the players his own age. And he wasn't just a great scorer and finisher—not many people realize what a good passer that James was."

"With Michael for instance, when I saw him I thought he'd be an ACC-type player," added Coach Guthridge. "But you couldn't tell he'd be a star. With James, you knew as an eighth-grader he'd be really, really good."

THE NEXT 'MAGIC'

James was such a good ball-handler and did so many things for Ashbrook High in Gastonia that it made Jim Braddock nervous. Those two were coming out of high school the same year, and Braddock didn't want to come to North Carolina if James was going to be installed as a 6-foot-9 point guard.

"I knew all about James when he was coming out of high school," Braddock said. "Some said he was going to be the next Magic Johnson. But Coach Smith told me during the recruitment

James Worthy in a relaxed moment on a friend's bike near our team's home that season, in Granville Towers on Franklin Street.
(Photo courtesy of David Daly)

process that they had signed Worthy, and he'd be our power forward. That made me want to come, because I wanted to go somewhere that we could win a national championship."

Those two were freshmen roommates and became good friends.

"I remember our freshman year, James didn't like to run," Braddock said. "When the coaches started making us do our sprints, he'd be saying stuff under his breath like, 'Is he ever gonna stop?' or 'I'm going to take that whistle from him.' He didn't like running the sprints, but it paid off. Also, when he got there, he wasn't a great defensive player. Coach Smith threatened him by telling him he'd put him on the bench, and he really buckled down after that."

WORTHY'S FIRST TWO YEARS

Worthy's freshman and sophomore seasons with us were plagued by injury. The guy we all called "Stick" started off with all sorts of promise. Early in his freshman season, he threw down a ferocious dunk over Kenny Dennard when we upset then-No. 1 Duke in Durham.

Midway through his freshman season, though, he slipped on a wet spot on the Carmichael Auditorium floor and shattered his ankle against Maryland. The crowd hushed as he was taken from the floor. That was the end of the season for James—he played in only 14 games for us in 1979-80.

Then, as a sophomore, James did play the entire season for our team that got to the NCAA final against Indiana, but his ankle had two metal screws and a 10-inch rod in it. It bothered him the whole season, especially on rainy days, although he never would complain to the coaches about it. But he had tendonitis, and we knew it hurt him some. He played and played well, averaging 14.2 points per game, but he wasn't quite as explosive as he could be.

"I was playing on a pretty bad ankle my entire sophomore season," James recalled.

But then he had an operation in the spring of 1981 that removed the hardware. And, as a junior, during our championship season, he was basically unguardable. Even though he drew more attention by leading us in scoring after Al Wood graduated, he still got better and more dominating in all facets of the game.

Remembered Chris Brust: "James Worthy was the best college basketball player I ever saw. Easy. Even now, after all these years, I still say that. Everyone of course assumes it would be Michael Jordan, but MJ elevated his game once he got to NBA. James was the best player in college. He could run, jump, shoot—he could do absolutely everything."

TWO ON ONE

In practice during the 1981-82 season, we often double-teamed James in drills to make life a little more difficult for him. Timo Makkonen was frequently assigned to James during those workouts.

"Back then, if I'd had a ton of bucks and had to bet it all on someone who was going to be the biggest star ever in the NBA, I would have bet it all on James Worthy," Makkonen said. "I took such a beating from him in practice. Lots of times we had to put two guys on James to give him what he needed. James was the engine of that team and its biggest talent. And he was really easy to talk to—a great personality."

Cecil Exum was one of the other players that would occasionally have to guard James in practice. "James was a hard-nosed player who, without a doubt, was the man. It was great watching him play and train—but he could never dunk on me."

WHOSE FINAL FOUR WAS IT?

Rick Brewer has been associated with North Carolina athletics for close to 40 years, mostly working as the school's sports information liaison to the media. He was the school's sports information director in 1982 and was the one who set up all of the players' and coaches' interviews that season.

"Worthy was one of those really class guys. Dean would often say he's a warrior," Rick recalled." He was a *man*. He was a college student, sure; but he didn't act like a college kid. He was a guy who already had the airs that he knew what he was doing, and he was way ahead of his time as far as knowing what happening.

James Worthy with his parents following the 1982 championship game. Note the net around his neck—he wore it for quite awhile. *(Photo by Hugh Morton)*

"Don't get me wrong," Brewer continued. "Michael Jordan is the best player I've ever seen; but that was James Worthy's tournament, and it was James Worthy's Final Four. He was the star. Michael hit the final shot, yes; but because of his incredible pro career, people don't talk much about how James really controlled that final."

Georgetown coach John Thompson said much the same thing in a *Washington Post* story more than a decade after the game was played.

"Jordan wasn't the one that was hurting us," Thompson told *The Post.* "That's the most misleading thing about that game. James Worthy killed us, not Michael Jordan. Michael Jordan killed us with the last shot, but James put them there [by scoring 28 points], so we were very much concerned about what would

Sam Perkins (41) and James Worthy were all smiles as they got to hold the 1982 NCAA championship trophy in the postgame locker room after our win over Georgetown. *(Photo by Hugh Morton)*

happen with James. They put the ball in the post and reversed it to the weak side; Michael went opposite, and stuck it in the basket."

IF HE HAD STAYED ...

How could James have not gone to the NBA after his junior year? You can't go higher than No. 1 in the NBA draft, after all. Virginia's Ralph Sampson decided to stick around for his senior year, and when he did that, it all but assured James he would be the No. 1 pick.

But James has thought about what would have happened himself a few times. "It would have been a lot of fun to have played one more year with Michael, Sam, Matt Doherty and everybody else," he said. "We would have been awfully tough to contend with."

"It would have been back-to-back championships," said Cecil Exum.

Doherty thinks it might have been, too. "Worthy's quickness and his footwork were amazing. He could get the ball to the goal quickly, and with great touch. He scored in a variety of ways and was equally as good with either hand—jump hooks, turnaround jumpers, dunks—you name it. James was tremendous. We never would have won the 1982 championship without him."

12

SAM THE MAN

Once you knew Sam Perkins, you loved him. He was a great guy, graceful both on and off the court. His famous 41-inch shirtsleeves meant that he wore No. 41 for us, and also that he played much bigger than his official 6-foot-9 height. We needed that. Our team really had no true center. In the NBA, Sam was a forward and would extend his career with a great knack for the three-point shot. Including the playoffs, he made 1,001 NBA-range threes during his 17-year career in the league.

But Sam played the No. 5 spot for us as a sophomore during that 1981-82 season. He had to guard Ralph Sampson for us. He had to block shots for us. He had to rebound and run the floor. He made it all look effortless, but it wasn't. Sam worked very hard to do what we needed and never caused a bit of a problem.

Some people called him "Silent Sam" because Perkins was comfortable being quiet, and also because there's a famous statue on the Chapel Hill campus of a soldier holding a rifle. The statue has long been nicknamed "Silent Sam" by Carolina students. If you went to Carolina, you know where "Silent Sam" stands, not far from Franklin Street. The monument was erected in 1913 as a tribute to the 321 Carolina alumni who died in the Civil War.

Our Sam was also quiet, and he could shoot whenever necessary. He was also a self-starter. When it came to game time, all that quietness was quelled. People used to say 'Sam's not running hard, he's not playing hard.' I'm here to tell you, if the game was on the line, we didn't have to worry about Sam. Believe that. You could count on Sam for a blocked shot, or for scoring, or being in the right defensive position. Sam was a gamer.

Like Lynwood Robinson, Sam was also really into music—both then and now. We really had two team deejays that season, although Lynwood was the one who had to carry the portable stereo on trips. Sam is now based in Dallas and has his own entertainment company, which puts on concerts, shows, and other music events. He specializes in rap, jazz, and R&B.

"I've always been into music," Sam said. "I deejayed a couple of parties in college for fraternities and sororities. That was long before the day of the CD. All I had on my desk at Granville was turntables. I didn't really have books on there."

Sam also hosts a basketball camp in Chapel Hill each summer, usually in June, and he's a world traveler. He has been to Africa on behalf of the NBA to do basketball clinics and spread goodwill. He's a great guy, and he and I remain close to this day.

SCRATCHING HIS KNEECAPS

Sam's long arms were legendary, even on our own team. All of us had heard by the time he enrolled at North Carolina that he could literally scratch his kneecaps while standing straight. According to our play-by-play announcer Woody Durham, Coach Eddie Fogler told Sam to go ahead and touch his kneecaps in that way when Sam first ducked his head to enter the basketball office as a freshman.

"Let's just get it over with," Fogler said.

Said Coach Fogler in his interview for this book: "I don't know if I actually did that, but I'm sure Woody remembers what I told him. And it sounds like something I'd do."

Chris Brust, my fellow senior on the 1981-82 team, remembers something about our team meals. "When we sat down to eat, all at a table together, Sam was the shortest guy," Chris said. "I'm serious. His torso was very short. The rest of him, though, was so long."

The postgame scene was far different after the 1981 NCAA title game, which we lost to Indiana. Here, Sam Perkins was alone with his thoughts in his locker after our loss. *(Photo by Hugh Morton)*

After the 1982 championship final, Sam Perkins had a few words with CBS.
(Photo by Hugh Morton)

NEW YORK STATE OF MIND

Like me, Sam was a New Yorker. He barely played basketball as a kid, and was raised as a Jehovah's Witness by his grandmother in Brooklyn. He didn't even play basketball as a sophomore on his high school team.

But a man named Herb Crossman—a recreation league coach in Brooklyn—discovered Sam and got him to start playing basketball. The two became friends, and Sam quickly proved to be a basketball prodigy. Crossman asked Sam's grandmother if he could become Sam's legal guardian and take him out of Brooklyn and to the suburbs of upstate New York. There, in the small town of Latham, New York, Sam could live with Crossman's family.

Sam's grandmother said yes. And so it was there that Sam really began his basketball career. He got so good so fast that he was invited to Colorado Springs, Colo., while still in high school to play in the U.S. Olympic Festival against some other national-level high school players.

It was in Colorado, during the summer of 1979, that Sam got to know James Worthy. That's also where Coach Dean Smith first saw Sam play and decided we had to recruit him.

A few months later, when Sam took his recruiting visit to North Carolina in November 1979, James was his host.

"James was really the guy who got me to go to North Carolina," Sam recalled. "I met him in Colorado, and from then on, I looked up to him. James was really the catalyst of our team in 1981-82. It wasn't Michael Jordan, although I know that's hard for people to believe now."

WORTHY'S PREDICTION

Worthy got very excited when he heard that Sam was coming to join us at North Carolina. Jim Braddock and James Worthy were roommates as freshmen, in 1979-80, and Jim still vividly remembers the two of them walking across campus to a class in April 1980. It was a beautiful spring day in Chapel Hill, and this is how Jim remembers the conversation.

"I just got through talking to Coach Smith on the phone," Worthy told Braddock. "We're signing Sam Perkins. Do you know how good he is? He's 6-feet-9, he can rebound, and he might be as good as you are shooting from 20 feet out."

"Ain't no way," Braddock said.

"Oh, yeah," Worthy said. "He can do everything. And with Perkins, before the two of us leave here, we're going to win a national championship."

"I'm going to hold you to that," said Braddock, laughing.

OFF THE BENCH

Sam was never one of those players who felt like he had to start. And he didn't for much of his freshman year—he came off the bench behind Pete Budko. Still, he played 30 minutes a game and averaged 14.9 points per game.

There was no hiding how good he was. He was Most Valuable Player of the 1981 ACC tournament—as a freshman! At that point in ACC tournament history, only Phil Ford had done that.

"And Sam wanted to give that honor up after the game," Coach Smith remembered. "He kept saying, 'I didn't do anything to deserve this—I just made a few layups and blocked a couple of shots.' It wasn't false modesty. That's the way he really was."

IRONING

When you talk to Sam's former teammates about his college habits 25 years later, it's amazing how many of them remember one thing he used to do in his spare time—ironing.

Sam liked to look neat, so he ironed a lot. It stuck in people's minds because of when he would do it. Remembered Jim Braddock: "Sam just wasn't a huge fan of basketball. On an off day, we'd all be watching a college basketball game in somebody's room, and Sam would be in his room ironing, or maybe going out with his friends to get an ice-cream cone."

"Sam really did iron a lot," Buzz Peterson said, chuckling.

"Sam reminded me of Bobby Jones," said Rick Brewer. "Like Bobby, basketball was no big deal to him when he wasn't playing it. They were both quiet off the court, too."

Said Lynwood Robinson: "Sam is the only great player I knew who didn't care that much about the game if he wasn't playing it.

He just showed up and played. He didn't really care who we played or what league they were in. We'd be watching some big game—maybe me, Michael, Buzz and Jimmy—and Sam would be either ironing or out there washing his car. Sam has always been eclectic. Offbeat. Off-center. And an absolute sweetheart of a guy."

"The Lanky Yank from New York became one of my best friends," laughed Cecil Exum. "And Sam was smooth off the court, too—no shortage of girls."

THE INSIDER

Sam really thought he could play anywhere on the court, and he could. He was a good ball-handler. It was so difficult to press us that season that hardly anyone ever tried—everyone could handle the ball. We could break a press with Sam and Worthy bringing the ball up court.

Said Sam of his role that year: "I just tried to work well with Worthy. My forte was a little half-hook, half-jump shot that I'd shoot with my left hand around the basket. I worked on that every day with Coach Guthridge. All of my shots came from the free throw line and inside it that year—although once the three-point line came into the ACC on an experimental basis the next season, I got to shoot that some, too. I would have liked to shoot more from outside on our 1982 championship team, but we had enough shooters; so I had to help maintain the middle."

SAM'S WARNING

Sam remembers that several of the older players used to tease Michael Jordan about sticking out his tongue so often while playing basketball. This was long before Jordan's tongue had become one of his signatures. Back in 1981-82, when Jordan was a freshman, it was more of an oddity than anything else.

"You're going to bite that thing one day, sticking it out like that," Sam said he told Michael once. And, Sam reports, Michael did. Jordan didn't hurt himself badly, but there was a little blood and, according to Sam, Jordan was a little embarrassed.

Here's a nice burst of emotion from Sam Perkins, who was sometimes unjustly criticized for not seeming to try hard enough because he looked so graceful on the court. Sam was such a gamer—he was always ready to play when it mattered. *(Photo by Sally Sather)*

PERKINS AS A PLAYER

Sam was a terrific player for the Tar Heels for four years, and so essential to our championship as well. He averaged 14.3 points and 7.8 rebounds in 1981-82—second on the team to Worthy in scoring and first in rebounds.

"Sam was a great teammate," said Jim Braddock. "He came across as someone who was kinda nonchalant on the court, but his exterior, his body language—he was just so smooth with everything he did. It never looked like he put forth massive energy because he made tough things look so easy. You couldn't really tell how fierce of a competitor he really was because of that smoothness. He reminded me a lot of Alex English."

Said James Worthy: "Sam was glue that held us together. At 6-feet-9, he played like he was seven feet tall. He was a dominant shot blocker [still second all-time in UNC history, to Brendan Haywood]. Sam went up against Sampson, Jim Johnstone at Wake Forest, and whomever else we needed him to stop inside. He was a defensive genius, and you always could count on him."

TRIVIA QUESTION

Woody Durham likes to ask this question of folks who believe they know their North Carolina basketball.

"I used to get people to guess wrong on it all the time," Durham said. "Now, though, I think I've asked it too much because people seem to get it right more often than wrong. The question is: 'Who is the only Tar Heel to rank in the top five on the school's all-time list in both scoring and rebounding?'"

The answer?

"Sam Perkins," Woody said. "Sometimes people forget how great of a player he really was here—a four-year player who contributed in a huge way from his freshman year onward."

In fact, Woody could rephrase the question and make it "top two" instead of "top five."

Sam ranks No. 2 all-time in points for North Carolina with 2,145. Only Phil Ford, with 2,290, scored more in a Tar Heel uniform.

The two big inside threats on our team—Sam Perkins and James Worthy—became very close. They got to know each other while both were still in high school. *(Photo by Sally Sather)*

Neither Michael Jordan nor James Worthy, who played only three years apiece at Carolina, are in the top 10 in scoring. Points aren't everything, of course. I still believe the best two Tar Heel players ever in college were Phil Ford and James Worthy. Michael, obviously, became the best pro.

In rebounding for North Carolina, George Lynch is No. 2, Billy Cunningham No. 3, Antawn Jamison No. 4, and Mitch Kupchak No. 5.

And the No. 1 all-time board man for North Carolina—with 1,167 rebounds?

Sam Perkins.

13

MICHAEL JORDAN

Everyone has a Michael Jordan story from 1982. We all knew him when he was very young—before the shoes, before the magazine covers, before the six NBA championships and the minor-league baseball, and the retirements, and the comebacks, and all the rest. We knew him first as a teenager—a raw, extremely competitive college freshman. He had hair then, and he was known as "Mike." Michael, in fact, will tell you, even today, that his name didn't really change from "Mike" to "Michael" until he hit "The Shot" in the championship game.

It's hard to believe now, but teams would actually *choose* to let Michael shoot jump shots against us rather than let James Worthy or Sam Perkins touch the ball inside.

Michael doesn't need much of an introduction, so I'll stop there. The stories in this chapter are all about Michael.

THE DUNK NO ONE SAW

As you know already, two incredible freshmen had huge roles in that 1982 title game—Jordan and Patrick Ewing for Georgetown.

But did you know Ewing once took an official recruiting visit to Chapel Hill? And Michael was here that weekend as well. Roy Williams, then our 31-year-old assistant coach and the current Tar Heels' head coach, supervised their visit. Coach Williams was walking Ewing and Michael over to a football game at Kenan Stadium.

On the way, the three of them decided to stop at Carmichael Auditorium, which is just a few hundred yards away from our football stadium. Here's how Coach Williams remembered the incident: "There's a little kid in Carmichael shooting, all by himself. I'm not sure how he got in there, but he did. Michael and Patrick are both in street clothes. The kid has no idea who either one of them are, of course—Patrick and Michael are both still in high school, and recruiting is nothing like it is today. But he can tell they probably play, because they're so big, and so he doesn't argue when Michael says, 'Hey kid, can I borrow that ball for a minute?'

"So Michael and Patrick go out on the court. Michael shoots one, with Patrick guarding him a little bit, and he makes it. Then Michael starts yapping at him, like we all know Michael will do. So this is getting Patrick fired up. Ewing gets the ball, and he starts dribbling, dribbling, backing Michael down. He gets in the lane. Then Patrick jumps up and dunks it *on Michael's head*. Then, before it gets any rougher, I say, 'Guys, let's get onto the football game.' The whole thing was no more than two minutes long, and I still don't know if that little kid really knows what he saw."

THE RECRUITMENT

It is a well-known true story that Michael was once cut from the varsity team at Wilmington (NC) Laney High. But by the time he was a junior, he was an awfully good player there. Lynwood Robinson, who was the same year as Michael, played for an opposing high school in eastern North Carolina and saw Jordan up close many times during those seasons.

"We went 5-2 against Michael when he was there," Lynwood said. "Once, we held him to seven points during his junior year. Usually, he'd get 25 or 30, but we'd win anyway. We had a more balanced team. I knew, even then, he was the best player I'd played against in high school. He was so long, and he played around the rim, and his shot was so soft, he never bricked it. Even when he missed, it just rimmed out. But never in a million years did I think he'd be as good as he got."

Michael Jordan with his father, James Jordan, following our 1982 championship-game win. I always thought Michael looked so much like his dad. *(Photo by Hugh Morton)*

Coach Bill Guthridge was the first of the North Carolina coaches to see Michael play. "A friend of mine called me from Wilmington and said there's a good player at Laney you ought to come down and look at. That was the first time we'd heard of him."

'So I went down and saw him and when I came back, I told Coach Smith we ought to offer him a scholarship," continued Guthridge. "I said he was an ACC-level player, but I don't know how good he was going to be—not like you knew with James Worthy by the time he was about 14 years old. Then, Michael was just a good athlete. But by his senior year, we knew Michael was going to be *good*—we didn't know how good. Anyone who said he was for sure going to be a great, great player then—or even after his freshman year—would be wrong or lying. But he had that unbelievable competitiveness, you could see that."

LURING BUZZ

"I actually gave a verbal commitment to Kentucky in August or September of 1980, just before my senior year began," remembered Buzz Peterson, who, as mentioned earlier, beat out Jordan for North Carolina high school player of the year during their senior season. "My high school coach in Asheville didn't like that too much. He called Roy Williams and told him, and Coach Smith was at my high-school gym the very next day. I wanted to play, of course, like every kid does. But I started thinking more about North Carolina again after that Coach Smith visit. Mike Pepper had just left. The guy I would have to beat out was from Wilmington, and he'd be a freshman, too.

"Little did I know how good Michael would be," Buzz continued. "We did know each other a little then, and he actually committed in November, well before me. He'd call me and say, 'When are you going to commit, too?' I didn't say I was coming to Chapel Hill for sure until January."

Buzz still felt fairly confident he could beat Michael out for the starting job until the two of them played together in a high school all-star game in the summer of 1981. "I had seen him play before, but suddenly he seemed like a totally different player," Buzz said. "He had a chip on his shoulder. He scored about 30 points and should have won the game MVP. He didn't, though—Adrian Branch got it instead. I knew that day Michael would be awfully hard to beat out for that starting job."

'HELP US A LITTLE'

When Tar Heel play-by-play announcer Woody Durham asked him before the 1981-82 season began how practice was going, Dean Smith said: "Pretty good. I think the youngster from Wilmington is going to help us a little."

Laughed Durham 25 years later: "That was one of the greatest understatements of all time."

PREDICTING THE FUTURE

Of all the basketball guys who saw Michael Jordan early during his freshman year, no one predicted the future better than Billy Cunningham. Cunningham was Dean Smith's first truly great player in the 1960s. In one stunning game, he had 48 points and 25 rebounds. When Dean Smith was getting hung in effigy on the Chapel Hill campus in 1965, Cunningham was the one who helped pull the effigy down. He would later win NBA championships as both a player (1967) and a coach (1983) for the Philadelphia 76ers.

In other words, Billy C knew something about basketball. Cunningham liked to go back to Chapel Hill sometimes in the early fall while he was coaching the 76ers, to watch Smith conduct practice and to get a read on the next batch of Tar Heels. He and Smith would look at each other's film and critique each other's players.

"So I went down to watch the Tar Heels practice before the 1981-82 season," Cunningham said. "And I saw Jordan awhile. I then said to Dean: 'He's going to be the greatest player who ever came out of here.'

"But Dean got mad at me," Cunningham continued, laughing. "You know how he is—he doesn't like to hear anything like that. To him, everybody is equal. And I said, 'Coach, coach. Just look at Michael. This isn't brain surgery—look at the way he plays.'"

PERKINS ON JORDAN

Sam Perkins was only a year older than Michael—he was a sophomore in the 1981-82 season, while Michael was a freshman. But their personalities were very different. Sam was "Easy Sam", "Quiet Sam."

And Michael? Let Sam tell you.

"Michael was a young freshman, but you couldn't tell him anything," Perkins said. "If you told him he couldn't shoot, that he shouldn't shoot, then he'd shoot. It's hard for people to remember this, but he really didn't have that great of a jump shot at the time. But Coach Gut [Bill Guthridge] had Michael working on things. He would work on his weaknesses until they became a strength. And even then he was uncanny around the basket—he had a knack for scoring there.

"What I remember a lot about 1981-82," Perkins continued, "was that Michael made the practices so interesting. His team didn't always win. But if he did win, he'd make sure you heard about it, afterward back at the dorm room and all night long. That was part of what he did, and the competition got fiercer at practice and made us all better."

Everyone remembers how intense Michael was at practice. "He played hard and worked harder," Cecil Exum said. "He was the ultimate gym rat."

THE TONGUE

Michael was sticking out his tongue during basketball games before he ever got to Chapel Hill.

Jordan was asked early in the 1981-82 season about the habit, and he said: "I've always played with my mouth open, I guess. I'm used to it. … I've never thought it was dangerous. Coach Smith told me before the season I probably ought to use a mouthpiece. But I didn't, and he didn't say anything else about it."

THE JUMPERS

Coach Smith remembers Jordan as a decent outside shooter during his freshman season—not the best, not the worst. He shot over 50 percent that season, as he did for all three of his seasons at Chapel Hill, but that was partly because he did so much of his damage very near the basket on his acrobatic drives.

Recalled Coach Smith in his interview for this book: "At the end of his fifth year in the NBA, I asked Michael when he thought he became a pure shooter. He said, 'After about four years as a pro, I knew if I had an open 15-footer, it was going to go in.' That's my definition of a 'pure shooter.' The open 15-footer doesn't go in every single time, but it always looks like it's going to."

WHAT 'THE SHOT' DID

Michael has said in many interviews over the years, including a recent one with my co-author, Scott Fowler, that the shot at the end of the Georgetown game changed his life. It gave him even more confidence, he said, and made him realize that he could win many more games because of his great ability and his great work ethic. "It kick-started everything for me," as Jordan says today.

"I was an unknown outside the state back then, although everyone in the state of North Carolina knew who I was," Jordan said.

"I think Michael was a good player up to that point. But then, after hitting that shot—his confidence made him great," said Lynwood Robinson. "He hit that shot, and then, he grew a couple of inches, and he put on 20 more pounds of muscle and man, it was over. He became the best player there ever was."

UNRECOGNIZABLE

Jordan was fairly anonymous, even by midseason of our championship year. Once, after an afternoon game that we had won at home, Michael was walking with his mother, Deloris Jordan, on the track behind Carmichael Auditorium.

According to *The Charlotte Observer*, a jogger passed by Jordan and, with no idea who he was asking, said: "Do you know if the Tar Heels won?"

"Yep," Jordan said. "They won."

We all were able to get some practice cutting down nets during our championship season. Doesn't Michael look young? *(Photo by Hugh Morton)*

PING-PONG AND CARDS

We had access to a pool table and a ping-pong table in the basement of Granville Towers, and Michael spent a lot of time hanging around both of those, challenging people.

"You really couldn't play a game of ping-pong with him—not if you beat him," Jim Braddock said. "I'd never seen a more fierce competitor. He would make you play him again, and again, until he beat you. I could beat him in ping-pong sometimes, although he became the best on the team. And he always wanted to bet a Coke on the game, or else the loser would have to run an extra sprint before practice. He thrived on pressure. He always wanted to add pressure to the equation, because he was better when something was on the line."

"Michael hated to lose at anything," chimed in James Worthy. "Basketball, backgammon, pool—it just ate him up. The guy was a true winner. If I'd have stayed one more season, it would have been great to play together with him—along with Sam Perkins and the rest of the guys—for one more season."

Added Ralph Meekins, one of our team managers in 1982: "Michael and I used to play 'Crazy Eights,' the card game, wherever and whenever we could. We'd play for a nickel a card. He never wanted to stop when he was losing."

Rick Brewer knew Jordan as a diehard competitor. "Michael wanted to win everything—golf, basketball, whatever. That's all that mattered. He is the second-most competitive person I've ever been around."

And who would be the first?

"Dean Smith," Brewer replied. "He hated to lose just as much as Michael did and maybe—although you'll find this hard to believe—a little more."

THE FRENCH QUARTER

After the Georgetown game, many of us walked around in small groups in the French Quarter, soaking it in. In one group was our freshman reserve Buzz Peterson, his high school coach, and Buzz's college roommate, Michael Jordan.

"That shot I hit—how big do you think that is, Buzz?" Michael asked.

"It's pretty big now," Buzz replied. "But you mark my words—as the years go on, it will get bigger and bigger."

EPILOGUE

WHERE ARE THEY NOW?

Although the 1981-82 season was a high point in all of our lives, certainly it wasn't the end of our lives. We all have gone on to many other things over the past 25 years. I was a college senior in 1982. I now live in Durham with my wife and two children and work as a financial advisor with Raymond James Financial Services.

Here's what we were able to find out about the others on that 1982 team and what they have done with their lives in the intervening years. I am proud of all of them, and I thank them from deep in my heart for their time and their cooperation with this book.

In alphabetical order:

JIM BRADDOCK is a teacher and a high school basketball coach at Hammond—a private high school in Columbia, South Carolina. He's worked there for the past nine years. Before that, he worked at a high school in Jacksonville, Florida. Jim has coached a half-dozen players who went on to college scholarships, including Alex English Jr., son of the former NBA star. Jim won a state championship at Hammond as a coach to go along with the national championship he won in college at UNC as a player.

Jim has never been married. "I guess I'm unlucky in love," Braddock said, laughing. "But I've been lucky in a lot of other things."

JOHN BROWNLEE played two years at North Carolina before transferring back to his homestate of Texas and becoming the Southwest Conference Player of the Year. "I couldn't get off the bench at Chapel Hill," Brownlee said, "but I still loved being there that season and loved being part of that national championship. It was such an inclusive team."

After graduating from Texas, Brownlee played for two years in Europe and then returned to the Lone Star State. He has a successful career in commercial real estate in the Dallas-Fort Worth area. Brownlee is married and has three children—two boys and a girl.

CHRIS BRUST, my old college roommate and fellow senior on the 1981-82 team, lives in Goldsboro, NC. He's a finance director at the Toyota-Scion dealership there.

Chris and his wife have a blended family that includes six kids, so he's a busy guy. Chris played basketball in Holland, Ecuador, and Puerto Rico before returning to the United States following the end of our college career. He still remembers our championship season fondly—and modestly.

"My role was to give guys like James Worthy and Sam Perkins a one- or two-minute break and not mess things up too badly while I was in there," Brust said.

In reality, Chris was a great player, but few people knew that because he had some serious injuries.

MATT DOHERTY has had a high-profile coaching career since he graduated from North Carolina in 1984. After assistant-coaching jobs at Davidson and Kansas, he has been the head coach at Notre Dame, North Carolina, Florida Atlantic, and now SMU.

At North Carolina, Matt replaced Bill Guthridge as the head coach in 2000 after Coach Guthridge retired. He had some great success there early, but in 2003, he was forced to resign under pressure. I wish it hadn't ended that way.

Now Matt has landed on his feet, and I'm sure he'll have great success for many years to come as a head coach. He and his wife, Kelly, have a son and a daughter.

CECIL EXUM, once a small-town kid from eastern North Carolina, has lived in Australia for the past 20 years. Following college, he became a star basketball player in Australia, where he played for 10 years and became famous enough to do a bunch of endorsements. He now owns a business in Melbourne, Australia, called Critique Basketball Promotions. It runs camps and clinics for basketball clubs and helps to train elite athletes. Cecil also does a lot of coaching and consulting.

"I call Australia a mini-USA," Cecil said. "They love everything American."

Cecil has been married for 20 years to Desiree Exum, who also graduated from UNC and now works for IBM. They have three kids, all of whom are excellent athletes. Jamaar, 12, and Dante, 10, are two of the top basketball players in Australia in their age groups. Dante's twin sister, Tierra, is a gymnast who has Olympic aspirations. The Exums love Australia and live in an area that Cecil describes as "… very similar to North Carolina—both beaches and mountains."

Of the sports scene in Australia, Cecil said: "We do get ESPN here—and we pay for it at $79 a month! The Australians love Australian Rules Football, which is very barbaric—no protective gear and a lot of injuries. Their second love is cricket, which is boring."

TIMO MAKKONEN has a close business relationship with Jordan. Timo works in Connecticut for an organization that specializes in restaurant management. It owns Burger Kings in Eastern Europe.

"Yes, we're selling hamburgers in Budapest," Makkonen said, laughing. "And we also do domestic restaurants here in the U.S. for Michael. We run the Michael Jordan Steak House at Grand Central Station in New York as well as a couple of other restaurants in which he has invested. We deal directly with him. It's basically his seed money and our sweat equity."

Timo obtained got his MBA from North Carolina and previously worked for the Hyatt hotels. He and his wife Mary, who is also a UNC graduate, have a 12-year-old daughter.

WARREN MARTIN has worked as a teacher and coach at the middle school and high school level in North Carolina for the past 14 years. Warren spent the 2005-06 school year as an eighth grade social studies teacher and the JV high school coach at East Chapel Hill. He and his longtime significant other, Debbie, have no children.

"I guess I was fated to do this," Warren said. "The people who helped me the most in life were my coaches and teachers. We really had a good year with some good kids this past season—we went 16-2 and undefeated in our conference. I'll always remember 1982 as the year I got to play with legends. For myself, Perkins and Worthy were my idols, and I was able to play alongside them."

BUZZ PETERSON is now the head basketball coach at Coastal Carolina. In his first season there, his 2005-06 team came within one point of reaching the NCAA tournament, losing to Winthrop in the Big South tournament final.

Buzz's playing career at North Carolina was hampered by injuries, but he rose rapidly through the coaching ranks. He was an assistant for three schools—including North Carolina State, where he wore a raspberry-red blazer each time the Tar Heels played the Wolfpack.

Buzz remembers his old college roommate, Michael Jordan, teasing him that he wouldn't cut it as a head coach. "You'll never be able to come down on anybody hard enough," Jordan told him. "You smile too much."

Buzz has succeeded, though. He has been head coach at Appalachian State, Tulsa, Tennessee, and now Coastal Carolina. He and his wife, Jan, have three children—Nicole, Olivia, and Rob.

LYNWOOD ROBINSON lives in the Chapel Hill area and "... does a little bit of everything," as he said. Lynwood has worked for Ham's restaurants in various management capacities for the past four years and also runs his own production company. He is filming a feature-length documentary on one of his childhood heroes, Phil Ford. Lynwood also has a collection of 3,000 vinyl records—the man has never stopped loving his music.

Although Lynwood transferred to Appalachian State midway through his college career, his heart stayed at North Carolina. "I'm 42 years old now, and the day Coach Smith offered me a scholarship was still one of the four or five greatest things that ever happened to me."

Lynwood is not married and has no children. "I want to be a father someday—just not yet."

MICHAEL JORDAN became the best basketball player in the game's history. After hitting the shot that won the 1982 championship, he became the best player in college basketball and then the best player in the NBA.

Michael won six NBA championships with the Chicago Bulls and was named the league's Most Valuable Player five times. Michael also launched the Air Jordan brand of shoes and became the most well-known athlete in the world. He now lives in Illinois.

In 2006, Michael bought into the NBA's Charlotte Bobcats as a part owner. In his new role, he will have the final say on all the Bobcats' basketball moves. He does not plan to move full-time to Charlotte from his home in Illinois but does plan to pop in frequently. Said Michael shortly after he bought a piece of the Bobcats: "I'm going to be in tune and I'm going to be paying attention. My ultimate responsibility is to try and get this basketball team to where it has to go."

He also said he won't be a figurehead with the Bobcats, nor someone who makes pitches to sell expensive suites in the Charlotte Bobcats Arena.

"I'm not a seller," Michael said. "My job here is to help provide a solid basketball team that sells itself. I'm not going to be part of a dog-and-pony show. That's not me. I want to go and build this team so the team supports itself."

SAM PERKINS now has his own entertainment company that puts on concerts all over America. Sam had a 17-year NBA career that ended in 2001. He now lives in Dallas and comes to Chapel Hill every summer to run a basketball camp.

"We had such a strong team in 1980-81—that one could have won the national championship, too," Sam said. "When we got home that season, Jimmy Black just told us all, 'Let's do this next year.' And we did it."

JAMES WORTHY became the first player on our 1982 team to reach the Basketball Hall of Fame, in 2003. "Big Game James" played his last game for us against Georgetown—he left UNC after his junior season and became the No. 1 overall draft pick in the NBA. He played all 12 of his NBA seasons with the L.A. Lakers, winning three NBA championships on the "Showtime" teams of the late 1980s.

James has stayed in California after his 1994 retirement from the NBA. He is single and the father of two teenaged daughters. He does TV work as an analyst on the Lakers' broadcasts and also hosts a half-hour sports show in Los Angeles. And, like the rest of us, our journey to the championship in 1982 is a trip he will never forget.

COACH EDDIE FOGLER, like the other two assistants on the 1982 North Carolina staff, went on to head his own program. Like me, Coach Fogler was a point guard at North Carolina and played in two Final Fours. He served on Coach Smith's staff for 15 years until 1986, when he became head coach at Wichita State. Fogler would then become a college head coach for the next 15 years—first at Wichita State, then at Vanderbilt and finally at South Carolina. He was conference coach of the year three times along the way and the national coach of the year once, at Vanderbilt in 1993.

In 2001, saying he was "tired," Coach Fogler resigned as head coach after eight years at South Carolina.

Five years later, at age 57, he is still involved in basketball. Coach Fogler and his family live in the Columbia area, and he broadcasts about 15 games per year on television as a college basketball analyst. He also does some basketball consulting and co-hosts a radio show based in Nashville.

"That 1982 season was really fun," Fogler said. "After 30 years as a coach at some level in college basketball, sometimes the games run together. I catch myself turning on ESPN Classic, seeing an old North Carolina game with me as an assistant, and wondering, 'Did we win this one or not?' I'm not like Coach Smith. I don't remember everything. But that 1982 team—it was unforgettable."

COACH BILL GUTHRIDGE still lives in Chapel Hill and keeps a small office next to Coach Smith's on the ground floor of the

Smith Center. After Coach Smith retired in 1997, Coach Guthridge took over the North Carolina program for the next three years.

In two of those three seasons, he directed the Tar Heels to the Final Four. By the time he retired in 2000, Coach Guthridge had played or coached in 14 Final Fours—more than any other person in NCAA history. Coach Guthridge was Coach Smith's right-hand man and chief assistant for an astonishing 30 years at UNC.

"I remember walking out on Bourbon Street in New Orleans in 1982 with my wife after we won," Guthridge said, "and just feeling so happy for the players and for Coach Smith. It was great—one of the real pinnacles of my time at North Carolina."

He posted a record of 80-28 in his three seasons as the Tar Heels' head coach.

COACH ROY WILLIAMS took over as North Carolina's head coach in 2003 after Doherty resigned. He directed the Tar Heels to the 2005 national championship, winning a thriller in the final over Illinois.

The part-time assistant on our team in 1982, he was hired by Kansas in 1988 to be the Jayhawks' head coach. Williams stayed there until 2003, turning down the Tar Heels' coaching job in 2000 before accepting it three years later. He has been the head coach of five Final Four teams—the first four at Kansas. Coach Williams and his wife, Wanda, have two grown children, Kimberly and Scott, who both live in the Charlotte area.

COACH DEAN SMITH, now 75 years old, still follows UNC basketball avidly after retiring in 1997. He was basketball coach at North Carolina for 36 seasons and won 879 games, more than any other men's basketball coach in Division I history. Our 1982 national championship was his first. He won a second national title in 1993.

Coach Smith has a small office in the basketball arena named after him and comes in most days when he's not traveling. He still loves to play golf. Although he claims his near-photographic memory isn't as good as it once was, those around him are still amazed at his powers of recollection. He and his wife, Linnea, live in Chapel Hill.

This is where we all started, and this shot brings back a lot of memories. When we huddled up in practice, that was Coach Smith's time he spoke, and we all listened carefully. *(Photo by Hugh Morton)*

APPENDIX

1981-82 SEASON STATISTICS

Player	FG-FGA	FG%	FT-FTA	FT%	REB	RPG	PF	AST	TO	BLK	STL	PTS	PPG
Worthy, J.	203-354	.573	126-187	.674	215	6.3	75	82	94	37	52	532	15.6
Perkins, S.	174-301	.578	109-142	.768	250	7.8	74	35	53	53	33	457	14.3
Jordan, M.	191-358	.534	78-108	.722	149	4.4	91	61	57	8	41	460	13.5
Doherty, M.	122-235	.519	71-92	.772	103	3.0	60	105	64	0	26	315	9.3
Black, J.	100-195	.513	59-80	.738	59	1.7	81	213	87	8	58	259	7.6
Braddock, J.	28-62	.452	10-12	.833	17	0.5	16	40	23	0	6	66	1.9
Brust, C.	23-37	.622	10-22	.455	56	1.7	17	14	18	0	85	6	1.7
Peterson, B.	16-41	.390	3-7	.429	14	0.5	10	16	4	0	4	35	1.2
Exum, C.	8-21	.381	3-11	.273	17	1.0	9	6	7	0	1	19	1.1
Robinson, L.	7-11	.636	1-5	.200	3	0.2	1	3	6	0	4	15	1.1
Barlow, J.	12-31	.387	4-9	.444	23	0.8	17	6	12	1	4	28	1.0
Martin, W.	7-15	.467	0-5	.000	16	0.8	7	1	5	2	1	14	0.7
Brownlee, J.	4-7	.571	1-5	.200	14	1.1	6	0	6	1	1	9	0.7
Makkonen, T.	0-0	.000	2-4	.500	4	0.3	7	1	2	1	0	2	0.2

1981-82 GAME-BY-GAME BREAKDOWN

Record: 32-2.
Home: 9-1. Away: 7-1. Neutral court: 16-0.
ACC regular-season champion; ACC tournament champion; NCAA champion.

Date	Opponent	Site	Score
November 28	Kansas	Charlotte	W, 74-67
November 30	Southern Cal	Greensboro	W, 73-62
December 3	Tulsa	Chapel Hill	W, 78-70
December 12	South Fla.	Chapel Hill	W, 75-39
December 19	Rutgers	New York	W, 59-36
December 26	Kentucky	East Rutherford, NJ	W, 82-69
December 28	Penn State	Santa Clara, CA	W, 56-50 (OT)

1981-82 GAME-BY-GAME BREAKDOWN (CONT.)

Date	Opponent	Site	Score
December 29	Santa Clara	Santa Clara, CA	W, 76-57
January 4	William & Mary	Chapel Hill	W, 64-40
January 6	Maryland	College Park, MD	W, 66-50
January 9	Virginia	Chapel Hill	W, 65-60
January 13	N. C. State	Raleigh	W, 61-41
January 16	Duke	Durham	W, 73-63
January 21	Wake Forest	Chapel Hill	L, 48-55
January 23	Ga. Tech	Atlanta	W, 66-54
January 27	Clemson	Chapel Hill	W, 77-72
January 30	N. C. State	Chapel Hill	W, 58-44
February 3	Virginia	Charlottesville	L, 58-74
February 5	Furman	Charlotte	W, 96-69
February 6	The Citadel	Charlotte	W, 67-46
February 11	Maryland	Chapel Hill	W, 59-56
February 14	Georgia	Greensboro	W, 66-57
February 17	Wake Forest	Greensboro	W, 69-51
February 20	Clemson	Clemson, SC	W, 55-49
February 24	Ga. Tech	Chapel Hill	W, 77-54
February 27	Duke	Chapel Hill	W, 84-66
March 5	Ga. Tech	Greensboro	W, 55-39
March 6	N. C. State	Greensboro	W, 58-46
March 7	Virginia	Greensboro	W, 47-45
March 13	James Madison	Charlotte	W, 52-50
March 19	Alabama	Raleigh	W, 74-69
March 21	Villanova	Raleigh	W, 70-60
March 27	Houston	New Orleans	W, 68-63
March 29	Georgetown	New Orleans	W, 63-62

Celebrate the Heroes of North Carolina Sports
in These Other Releases from Sports Publishing!

Tales from the Tar Heel Locker Room (Updated and Revised Edition)
by Ken Rappoport
• 5.5 x 8.25 softcover
• 220 pages
• photos throughout
• $14.95

North Carolina Tar Heels: 2005 NCAA Champions
by *The Raleigh News & Observer*
• 8.5 x 11 hardcover and softcover
• 128 pages
• color photos throughout
• $19.95 (hard)
• $14.95 (soft)

Tales from the Duke Blue Devils Hardwood
by Jim Sumner
• 5.5 x 8.25 hardcover
• 200 pages
• photos throughout
• $19.95

North Carolina Tar Heels: Where Have You Gone?
by Scott Fowler
• 6 x 9 hardcover
• 192 pages
• photos throughout
• $19.95

David Thompson: Skywalker
by David Thompson with Sean Stormes and Marshall Terrill
• 6 x 9 hardcover
• 250 pages
• eight-page photo insert
• $22.95

Tales from the Wake Forest Hardwood
by Dan Collins
• 5.5 x 8.25 hardcover
• 200 pages
• photos throughout
• $19.95

Lowe's Motor Speedway: A Weekend at the Track
by Kathy Persinger
• 8.5 x 11 hardcover
• 128 pages
• color photos throughout
• $24.95
• Includes bonus CDracecard!

Legends of N.C. State Basketball
by Tim Peeler
• 8.5 x 11 hardcover
• 160 pages
• photos throughout
• $24.95

Tales from the Carolina Panthers Sideline
by Scott Fowler
• 5.5 x 8.25 hardcover
• 200 pages
• photos throughout
• $19.95

Tales from Pinehurst
by Robert Hartman
• 5.5 x 8.25 hardcover
• 200 pages
• photos throughout
• $19.95

All books are available in bookstores everywhere!
Order 24-hours-a-day by calling toll-free **1-877-424-BOOK (2665).**
Also order online at **www.SportsPublishingLLC.com.**